Modern Flavors of Arabia

MODERN FLAVORS

of

Arabia

Recipes and Memories from My Middle Eastern Kitchen

SUZANNE HUSSEINI

Photography by PETRINA TINSLAY

appetite

by RANDOM HOUSE

Library and Archives of Canada Cataloguing in Publication is available upon request

ISBN: 978-0-449-01561-2

Photographer: Petrina Tinslay
Food stylist: Alison Attenborough
Printed and bound in China

Published in Canada by Appetite by Random House,
a division of Random House of Canada Limited

www.randomhouse.ca

10 9 8 7 6 5 4 3 2 1

I long for my mother's bread,
my mother's coffee,
my mother's touch . . .

— *Mahmoud Darwish*

To my father,
who taught me to be a proud Arabian.

To my mother,
thank you for the love you put in every meal.
Your love lives on in my kitchen.

contents

dessert

introduction

My family immigrated to Canada when I was very young. I remember arriving in the middle of the winter and seeing snow for the first time.

A new beginning, where I had to learn a new language, make friends and get used to wearing mittens and boots. While all of this was challenging at times, my constant comfort was coming home to a kitchen filled with the most enticing smells, lovingly created by my mother. Our kitchen was the heart of our home. She would pack my school lunch with sandwiches made from homemade pita bread, filling them with hummus (which was not yet a household word in North America!), labneh, falafel and za'atar. My classmates, being curious, wanted to know where I was from. "You tell them you are *Arrrrabian*," my father advised, accentuating the *r*. But this answer only made them want to know more. The questions followed: "Is your father a sheikh?" "Does he have camels?" "Is he rich?" They were relentless. I was only too happy to invite these inquisitive friends home for lunch. They tasted my mother's cooking and, of course, loved it. The teasing eventually stopped, my "exotic" lunches became a hit and soon I was filling daily requests for falafel. I learned at age seven that we all share one thing and that is a love for food.

Much has been written about the legendary hospitality of the Arabs and our love of good food. Eating is an integral part of our life. We take it very seriously. For us, the age-old tradition of breaking bread is an honorable experience. This cookbook is my passionate attempt to showcase the diverse cuisine I grew up with, a cuisine that encompasses the Eastern Mediterranean, North Africa and the Middle East, a sophisticated food culture that has evolved over hundreds of years and was deeply influenced by the great Persian and Turkish civilizations. With the region situated at the crossroads of the spice route, Arabic cuisine naturally flourished and spread: the Arabs of long ago took their newly found ingredients – pine nuts, eggplants, pistachios, sugar, sesame, saffron, cinnamon, rice – and their farming and irrigation skills to places like Spain and Sicily. Sicilian cooking still uses so many Arabic ingredients and methods. Recently, I've been struck by how many well-known TV chefs are now looking to the Middle East for inspiration, incorporating ingredients such as sumac, harissa, tahini, saffron, rosewater and pomegranate molasses.

While the evolution of food traditions continues to fascinate me, this book is not meant to be a historical account of Arabic cooking. Rather, it is a collection of recipes I grew up with, the foods my mother cooked for our family, the dishes that brought comfort and joy to our hearts. One of the best skills I learned from my mother was to cook, as she would say, "with my eyes," and to keep tasting along the way. She always allowed us to experiment in the kitchen, even if it meant making a mess. This gave me the confidence to cook with no fear. Even though my attempts weren't always successful, she would taste it and say, "It is better than mine." She, incidentally, had an amazing talent for "cracking the code" of any dish she tasted in a restaurant, re-creating a better version of it at home the next day.

Over the years of eating at my mother's table, of teaching cooking classes, of gracing my own table with enthusiastic, food-loving friends and of simply cooking for my own family, I've learned so much about other cultures, exchanged many recipes and simply savored good times. This book is the result.

The dishes that follow are divided into five chapters, Breakfast being the first, followed by Mezze, Lunch, Dinner and lastly Dessert. I want to share with you the foods and the times they are typically eaten. Use these recipes as a guide, but follow your instincts and your senses, too. Cooking is a delicious adventure!

Suzanne

cook's notes

I am not rigid about measurements. My approach to cooking is relaxed. Use the recipes in this book as a guide and follow your instincts. Cooking is a sensual experience; all of the senses are present when you are cooking. If I do measure I just use standard ½-cup and 1-cup measurements. I find it easier. I use pinches and handfuls often. I could not measure herbs so a handful seems more real to me.

Feel free to use my recipes as a guideline bearing in mind my suggestions and then make it your own by increasing and decreasing an ingredient. Just read through the recipe entirely before making it.

- I certainly have my share of fancy utensils and favorite Le Creuset pots that I love to cook in, but truly good home-cooked Arabic meals are made with few tools and lots of love and soul. That said, it doesn't hurt to have a few indispensable gadgets like a food processor to make some jobs a breeze.

- There is no replacement for a mortar and pestle to crush garlic and onions and expose the scents of spices.

- I like to use a handheld electric mixer to really get at my ingredients.

- Long before there were spoons, there were hands, and they are our best tools. Don't be afraid to get in and touch the food. Taste as you cook and smell and taste again to experience the process and the changes that occur.

Throughout the book:

- eggs are large and organic

- chicken is free range and organic

- oranges and lemons are unwaxed when a recipe asks for zest (scrub well with warm water before zesting)

- olive oil is extra virgin

Tips:

- I toast nuts like almonds, pistachios and pine nuts and store them in the fridge in sealed glass jars.

- I fry my own Arabic croutons and store them in sealed bags in the freezer.

- I clarify my own butter (see page 181) and keep it in a sealed jar in the fridge.

- I like the mildness of sea salt.

- I make simple syrup (see recipe on page 181) and keep it in a sealed jar to have on hand for when I have the urge to make something sweet.

breakfast

Breakfast does not have to be complicated. It could be as simple as a perfectly
fried egg sprinkled with tart sumac and fresh thyme with a bowl of olives on the side.
Mornings are a nice time to do some light baking, whether it is scones sweetened with dates,
savory cheese buns or a perfectly baked egg nestled in sautéed spinach. The aromas will
put a smile on anyone's face.

Listening to the sweet angelic voice of Fairouz on the stereo while savoring a fresh cup of coffee
is the way I start my mornings. I love laid-back weekend mornings when breakfast is the main
event. Breakfast at my mother's table was always a medley of textures and flavors.
And I've carried on that same tradition.

Besides the choice of breakfast recipes in this section, feel free to include dishes from the
mezze chapter on your breakfast table.

Manaqeesh za'atar is a common snack all over the Arab world and can be eaten anytime of the day. Basically it is a flatbread with a dry za'atar and olive oil topping. There are endless choices of toppings. Manaqeesh is the generic name for these breads. I love to combine fresh wild thyme, green onions and tomatoes as an alternative topping. Caramelized onions, spinach, labneh, eggs and cheese are also delicious options.

Cheese and Za'atar Flatbread

Makes 8 small flatbreads

3½ cups flour • 1 Tbsp salt • 1 Tbsp sugar • 1 tsp instant dry yeast • 2 Tbsp olive oil
1¼ cups lukewarm water • 1 cup za'atar (spice mixture with dried thyme) • ½ cup extra virgin olive oil
1 lb akkawi cheese, mozzarella or a combination of both (or of any white cheese you like)

In a large bowl mix the flour, salt, sugar and yeast. Pour in the 2 Tbsp oil and the water gradually. Mix to form a dough. Turn out onto a floured surface and knead for 5 minutes until the dough becomes elastic and smooth. Place in a greased bowl and cover with a damp cloth. Leave to rise in a draft-free place for 1½ hours until it doubles in size. Cut the dough into 8 equal parts and shape into balls. Dust with a little flour and cover with a towel. Leave to rest for an additional 30 minutes.

Preheat the oven to 400°F.

Combine the za'atar and the ½ cup olive oil to make the topping. Shred the cheese and leave aside.

On a floured surface, flatten each ball and with a rolling pin roll into a circle of approximately 6–8 inches. Place on greased baking sheets and spread the za'atar/oil mixture on some of the circles leaving a ½-inch border. Do the same for the cheese flatbreads. Use your fingers to spread the fillings evenly. Pinch and crimp the edges to create a decorative border. Bake in the preheated oven for 10–12 minutes until lightly golden, and serve hot.

I had a ritual of making these buns on Fridays as an after-school snack for my children. Friends would pop in unexpectedly as I was pulling them out of the oven. The surprise visits became regular and always on a Friday. I later discovered that my son, Mahmoud, was spreading the word to come to our house to eat because "my mum makes so much food, plenty for everyone." Well, he was right. And I always loved those moments in my kitchen with my children and their friends.

Halloumi/Feta Cheese Bread Rolls

Makes 9 rolls

**2 cups flour • ½ tsp salt • 1 Tbsp sugar • 1 Tbsp instant dry yeast • 1 cup lukewarm water
½ cup yogurt • ¼ cup extra virgin olive oil**

**3–4 oz halloumi cheese, shredded • 2 oz Parmesan cheese, grated • 3–4 oz feta cheese, crumbled
½ handful fresh thyme, stems removed, chopped • ¼ cup fresh mint, chopped • 1 Tbsp olive oil • ¼ cup sesame seeds**

Place the flour in a large bowl with the salt, sugar and yeast. Stir to combine. Add the water, yogurt and ¼ cup oil and mix to form a dough. Turn out onto a floured surface and knead for 10 minutes until the dough becomes smooth and elastic. Put back into the bowl, cover with a damp cloth and leave to rise in a dark draft-free place for 1½ hours.

Scatter all the cheeses and herbs on the dough and knead gently to incorporate. Divide and form the dough into 9 equal-sized balls and place side by side in a parchment-lined 9-inch-square baking pan. Cover with a damp cloth and leave to rise again for 30 minutes.

Preheat the oven to 400°F. Brush the risen buns with 1 Tbsp olive oil, sprinkle sesame seeds on top and bake for 15 minutes until lightly golden. Serve hot straight from the oven.

A frittata with buttery sweet eggplant in the center. The mint is the right herb to complement the eggplant's mildness and the nuts add a sweet crunch. A dish I enjoy anytime, breakfast, lunch or dinner, with a nice salad.

Eggplant Frittata

4 servings

3 eggplants • ¼ cup olive oil and peanut oil, mixed
1 onion, finely chopped • 6 cloves garlic, minced
3 Tbsp olive oil • 8 organic eggs • ¼ cup milk • 1 tsp nutmeg
salt and pepper • ¼ cup parsley, chopped
¼ cup fresh mint, chopped • ½ cup toasted pine nuts,
plus more to garnish

Preheat the oven to 400°F.

Peel and slice the eggplant into about ¾-inch rounds. Brush both sides with ¼ cup oil and place on a baking sheet. Roast in the hot oven until golden. Turn halfway through roasting. Remove and set aside to cool. Leave the oven on while you prepare the frittata. In a large ovenproof frying pan sauté the onion and garlic in the olive oil until soft. Cut the eggplant into cubes and add to the pan, stirring gently. Beat the eggs, milk, seasonings, parsley and mint. Pour over the eggplant mixture. Sprinkle some of the pine nuts on top. Cook on medium heat until eggs just begin to set. Place the frying pan in the hot oven to finish cooking. The frittata will become fluffy. Cook for no longer than 5 minutes. Remove the frittata from the oven, garnish with more pine nuts and slice into wedges.

Serve with a fresh tomato and mint salad.

Tomato and Mint Salad

4 servings

2 cups cherry tomatoes, sliced in half
2 green onions, sliced thin (whites only)
juice of 1 lemon • ¼ cup fresh mint, chopped
salt and pepper • extra virgin olive oil

Toss all the ingredients together and drizzle with olive oil. Serve immediately.

A nice way to serve eggs for breakfast. They can be prepared all at once ahead of time. An unexpected surprise waits at the bottom. Not knowing is half the fun! Here I've made a spinach filling, but feel free to put in any of the other additions I suggested.

▨ ▨

Middle Eastern Baked Eggs

6 servings

6 organic eggs • 2 Tbsp crème fraîche (or cream) • salt and pepper • unsalted butter, to coat ramekins

Sautéed Spinach Filling

2 Tbsp olive oil • 2 cloves garlic, sliced thinly • 1 small onion, diced
4 cups fresh, washed baby spinach leaves • 1 tsp nutmeg • 1 tsp sumac • salt and pepper
toasted hazelnuts, chopped, to garnish • toasted pine nuts, to garnish

Additions: *fresh thyme, fresh tarragon, chives, za'atar, feta cheese, dukkah (see page 53), sautéed potatoes with fresh cilantro*

In a large frying pan sauté the garlic and onion in olive oil until soft. Slice the spinach coarsely and add to the onions. Stir to combine and allow to wilt and cook for 5 minutes. Sprinkle in the nutmeg, sumac, salt and pepper. Taste to adjust the seasonings. Allow to cool completely.

Heat the oven to 375°F. Butter six ½-cup ramekins. Place the sautéed spinach mixture and any of the additions in the bottom of each ramekin.

Crack an egg into each ramekin. Put 1 teaspoon of crème fraîche beside, not touching, the egg yolk. Season with salt and pepper. Put the ramekins in a deep-sided baking pan. Pour hot water into the pan to reach halfway up the sides of the ramekins. Bake for 5–6 minutes until cooked but slightly wobbly in the center. Serve with toasted pita wedges and garnish with toasted hazelnuts and pine nuts and/or more sumac.

Crispy Pita Wedges

Preheat oven to 375°F. Split 6 small pita breads. (You will have 12 rounds.) Stack 3 at a time and use a pizza cutter to cut into triangles. Spread out on a baking sheet. Brush lightly with olive oil. Season with sea salt and black pepper. Bake until golden and crisp. Store any extra in a sealable container.

I love this cheese. Its saltiness is a nice foil to many sweet items, including watermelon and grapes.
By frying it, its blandness is elevated to a delightful bite of crisp on the outside and soft on the inside.
A sweet tea is definitely the drink to have with halloumi cheese. I also serve it as part of a mezze spread and often in salads.

Fried Halloumi Cheese

4 servings

1 lb halloumi cheese • flour • 2 Tbsp clarified butter

Slice the cheese so that you have 4 rectangular slices, and cut each slice into 2 triangles. Blot dry on a paper towel and dredge each piece in some flour. In a large nonstick frying pan heat the butter and fry the halloumi until golden on both sides.

Serve immediately while hot. Fresh tomatoes and olives on the side are a must. Fresh herbs like mint and thyme go well with this cheese.

Fattet hummus is a layered dish traditionally eaten for breakfast. With each spoonful you taste the crunch of the bread, the warm earthiness of the chickpeas, the tangy cool yogurt and the sweet richness of the nuts. It's a perfect parfait of flavors and textures.

Chickpeas with Yogurt Topping and Pita Croutons (Fattet Hummus)

6 servings

2 cups cooked chickpeas, rinsed and drained if canned
2 cups full-fat yogurt • 3 Tbsp tahini
3 cloves garlic, mashed • juice of 1 lemon
2 cups pita croutons • ½ cup toasted chopped pistachios
½ cup toasted slivered almonds • ½ cup toasted pine nuts

In a saucepan, heat the chickpeas over medium heat and set aside, keeping warm.

To make the sauce, put in a bowl the yogurt, tahini and half of the garlic. Mix well until creamy and set aside. Mix the remaining garlic with the lemon juice to make a dressing, and set aside.

In 6 individual small clear glass bowls, place a layer of the pita croutons in the bottom and drizzle a little of the garlic-lemon dressing on top. Drain and spoon some hot chickpeas on the crispy bread layer. Next, pour on the prepared yogurt sauce. Garnish with all of the nuts or pick one you especially like. Serve immediately.

Pita Croutons

2 large pita breads • ½ cup peanut oil

Split the pitas and pull apart to make 4 rounds. Cut up into small squares. Heat the peanut oil (not too hot) in a large frying pan. Fry half the amount of bread until golden and crisp. Remove and drain on absorbent paper. Fry the second batch the same way. Store any extras in sealed bags and keep in the freezer for future use.

My daughter Mimi went through a phase where she would only eat za'atar sandwiches for her school lunch. I used pita bread, buns, crackers and anything I could think of to deliver her favorite snack in a different way. This is how these croissants were born. It's a soft bread dough filled with za'atar and rolled like a croissant. I still make a big batch and freeze extras for when her friends Tala, Gaby and Lana come to visit. They are a welcome treat for breakfast or as an afternoon snack.

Za'atar Croissants

Makes 48 croissants

6 cups flour • 3 Tbsp powdered milk • 1 tsp salt • 1 Tbsp sugar
2 Tbsp instant dry yeast • 2 Tbsp olive oil • 2½ cups lukewarm water
1 cup za'atar (spice mix with dried thyme) • ¾ cup olive oil

¼ cup milk • ¼ cup sesame seeds

In a large bowl, put 4 cups of the flour, milk powder, salt, sugar and yeast and stir to combine. Add the 2 Tbsp oil and water and whisk together. Mix well. Add the remaining flour but only enough to make the dough come together. On a floured surface knead for 5 minutes. Place the dough back in the bowl and brush with a little olive oil. Cover with a damp cloth and leave to rise for 1½ hours until it doubles in size.

Preheat the oven to 400°F.

Mix the za'atar and the ¾ cup olive oil to make a paste. Set aside.

Divide the dough into 6 portions. Roll out one portion on a floured surface to form an 8-inch circle. With a knife, cut 8 triangles of equal size (like cutting a pizza). Put a spoonful of the za'atar and oil mixture in the center of the large part of each triangle. Roll up away from you starting from the large side toward the pointed end of the triangle to make a croissant. Place on a baking sheet that has been lightly greased with vegetable oil. Brush each croissant with a little milk and sprinkle some sesame seeds on top. Bake in the hot oven until lightly golden, approximately 15 minutes.

I like crepes more than pancakes since they are much lighter. This is a take on the well-known atayef bil ashta, which is basically a mini crepe folded in half, filled with clotted cream and drizzled with rose-flavored syrup. For a lighter option, use ricotta cheese. This is a great breakfast dish, with which I like to serve mangoes or strawberries. When in season, figs or apricots are a delicious alternative.

Mango and Ricotta-Filled Crepes with Rose Syrup

Makes 15 crepes

1 cup flour • 3 Tbsp sugar • pinch of salt • 2 eggs • 1⅓ cups milk • ½ cup heavy cream
½ cup ground pistachios • ½ tsp vanilla • ½ tsp orange blossom water • ¼ cup clarified butter

2 ripe mangoes • 1 cup rose syrup (see recipe on page 181)

Ricotta Filling
1 lb ricotta cheese • zest of 1 orange • ½ cup honey
½ cup pistachios, chopped, reserving some for garnish

Peel and slice the mangoes and put aside.

Mix the ricotta cheese, orange zest, honey and nuts and keep in the fridge while you make the crepes.

To make the crepe batter, put flour, sugar and salt in a bowl. Add the eggs and whisk well. Stir in half the milk to incorporate, then add the rest of the milk and cream to make a creamy batter. Stir in the pistachios and leave to rest for at least 1 hour.

Add the vanilla and orange blossom water and stir to mix. Brush a crepe pan or any nonstick frying pan lightly with clarified butter and heat. Using a ladle, pour a little batter and tilt the pan to cover thinly. Cook for 1 minute until little holes appear and turn over to cook for half a minute more. Place the cooked crepes on a platter, stacking them with wax paper separating the layers.

Place some filling and a few slices of mango in the middle of each crepe and fold twice. Drizzle with rose syrup and garnish with chopped pistachio nuts. Serve.

Foul m'dammas is a dip traditionally eaten for breakfast, but it can also be a healthy protein-packed snack for anytime of the day. Scoop morsels with pita bread and enjoy with sliced tomatoes, sliced cucumbers and fresh mint on the side.

❖ ❖

Fava Bean Dip

4 servings

10 oz (about 1½ cups) canned fava beans (also sold as "broad beans")
2 cloves garlic, mashed • juice of 1 lemon • 1 tsp cumin
1 hot red chili, seeded and chopped • sea salt
½ cup parsley, chopped • 1 tomato, diced
extra virgin olive oil

In a saucepan heat the fava beans and the liquid from the can until it boils, and then remove the saucepan from the heat. Using a slotted spoon, remove the fava beans from the water and place in a bowl. Add the mashed garlic, lemon juice, cumin and chili. Lightly mash the mixture, keeping most of the beans whole. Season with salt. If the mixture is too thick add some of the cooking water to loosen it. To serve, place the fava bean dip in a bowl, garnish with the parsley and diced tomatoes and drizzle with the olive oil.

Serve hot with fresh pita bread, along with sliced tomatoes, hot peppers and fresh mint on the side.

The ultimate combination of fried eggs, sausages na'aniq and hash browns. The familiar can be comforting but so is waking up your taste buds to new flavors. The eggs are sprinkled with tangy sumac, the sausages are bursting with a blend of special spices and the hash browns are crisp and infused with cilantro. The texture of these tasty sausages is enhanced with pine nuts. These sausages also make a good mezze option.

Arabic-Style Fried Eggs

4 servings

2 Tbsp clarified butter (or olive oil)
8 organic eggs • salt and pepper • 1 Tbsp sumac

Heat the butter (or oil) in a large cast-iron or nonstick frying pan. Crack the eggs one by one into the hot pan. Season with salt and pepper. Sprinkle the sumac on top. Cook the eggs to your liking.

Arabic-Style Hash Browns

4–6 servings

4 large russet potatoes • 2 cloves garlic, mashed
½ cup fresh cilantro, chopped • 1 tsp paprika
½ tsp cayenne pepper • salt and pepper
¼ cup peanut oil

Peel and grate the potatoes and place in a sieve to drain. Put in a clean dishtowel to squeeze out any remaining moisture. Place in a bowl and add the garlic, cilantro, paprika, cayenne pepper, salt and pepper and mix well.

In a large nonstick frying pan heat the oil, and place spoonfuls of the potato mixture and flatten with the back of a spoon. Leave to fry until golden brown for about 3 minutes. Turn over to brown the other side. Serve hot with the fried eggs.

Spicy Sausages (Sausages Na'aniq)

Makes 30 sausages

1 lb finely ground lamb, not too lean
(shoulder cut is fine)
½ tsp ground ginger • 1 tsp cinnamon
1 tsp nutmeg • 1 tsp allspice • ½ tsp cloves
1 Tbsp sugar • 1 clove garlic, mashed
½ tsp mahlab ground with ½ tsp salt
½ cup pine nuts • 2 Tbsp pomegranate molasses
¼ cup olive oil for frying
1 lemon, half of it cut into wedges to garnish • salt and pepper
pomegranate molasses, to garnish

Have your butcher grind the meat twice so it has a smoother texture and use meat that has some fat like the shoulder. The flavor is much better. Add all of the spices, mashed garlic, pine nuts and pomegranate molasses. Cover with plastic wrap and refrigerate for 4 hours to allow the flavors to mingle. Shape into mini-sized sausages, wetting your hands in cold water to prevent sticking.

In a large frying pan heat the olive oil and fry the sausages until brown all over. Squeeze a little lemon juice near the end of cooking. Toss to coat all of them. Serve the sausages hot with a lemon wedge on the side and a drizzle of pomegranate molasses.

A breakfast treat your family and friends will never forget. The aroma of hot scones just coming out of the oven is like nothing else.
(And yes, ¼ cup baking powder is correct – there are no eggs in this recipe, and baking powder is the only raising agent.)
I always have mascarpone cheese lightened with cream and flavored with orange zest on the side. I've added Arabic flavors
to this well-known British pastry. It will make you a morning person again.

Date and Orange Scones

Makes 16 scones

4½ cups flour • 1 cup unsalted cold butter, cut into small cubes • 1 cup sugar
¼ cup baking powder • 1 tsp cardamom • 1 tsp nutmeg • zest of 1 orange
2 cups pitted and chopped dates • 1 cup heavy cream • ¾ cup milk

eggwash (2 eggs beaten with 1 Tbsp milk) • muscovado sugar

Preheat the oven to 400°F. In a large bowl put the flour and cold butter cubes. Using your fingers and working fast to keep the mixture cold, rub the butter into the flour until you get a crumbly consistency. Add the sugar, baking powder, cardamom, nutmeg, orange zest and the dates. Mix with your hands to distribute evenly. Pour in the cream and milk and mix with a spatula using a light hand. A light touch ensures that the scones will be light and fluffy. Turn out the soft, sticky dough on a floured surface. Fold over the dough a couple of times to shape into a square, dusting with a little flour. Roll out to about a 1-inch thickness.

I use a 2-inch-square cookie cutter to cut the scones, but feel free to use other shapes. Gather the remaining dough, reroll and cut. Lay scones on a baking tray lined with parchment paper, keeping them 1 inch apart. Brush with eggwash. Sprinkle each scone with the muscovado sugar. Bake in a preheated oven for 15–20 minutes until puffed and golden on top. They are sweet enough to eat plain. Delicious with mascarpone spread, jam or honey.

Mascarpone Cheese Spread

1 cup mascarpone cheese • ½ cup heavy cream
zest of 1 orange • 2 Tbsp honey

Mix all of the ingredients in a bowl and serve alongside the hot scones.

Labneh starts out as laban, which is the Arabic word for yogurt. Labneh is thick and silky and a perfect dip when you add different herbs or vegetables to it. The following are three of my favorite combinations. You can find ready-made labneh at many Middle Eastern grocers. Some are good but homemade is best and so easy to make! Just plan to start making it two days before serving.

Labneh Three Ways

4-6 servings each

1 cup labneh • ½ cup fresh mint, stems removed, chopped
pinch of sea salt

1 cup labneh • ½ handful fresh thyme, chopped
pinch of sea salt • 2 Tbsp toasted sesame seeds

1 cup labneh
10 kalamata olives, pitted and chopped coarsely
10 green olives, pitted and chopped coarsely
pinch of sea salt

extra virgin olive oil

Refer to the recipe on page 181 if you are using homemade labneh.

Make each version of labneh by combining the ingredients. Taste to add more salt if necessary. Spread each labneh combination in a small, shallow plate.

With the back of a spoon make indentations for the olive oil, to be poured over the labneh before serving. Eat with crispy pita wedges (see recipe on page 9) or as a dip for vegetables.

A lovely bread to have with breakfast instead of toast. These little thyme (za'atar) stars are traditionally made with a lot of oil but I cut back to make them more fluffy. The semolina gives them a crispy texture. I use the wild thyme commonly available in the Middle East (see page 183), but you may substitute fresh oregano (which is closely related to wild thyme) or a decreased amount of regular thyme. These stars are nice to eat with labneh or any white cheese like feta or halloumi. I always have containers of these in the freezer ready for when Mimi's friends drop by.

Fresh Thyme Stars

Makes 24 stars

4 cups flour • 1 cup semolina or cornmeal
1 tsp baking powder • 1 tsp salt
1 Tbsp sugar • 1 Tbsp instant dry yeast
½ cup olive oil • 2½ cups lukewarm water
7 handfuls fresh wild thyme (or fresh oregano), washed, drained and stems removed
1 tsp sea salt • olive oil, for brushing

In a large bowl put the flour, semolina, baking powder, salt, sugar and yeast. Mix well. Gradually add half of the oil and all the water and mix to form a dough. It should be soft and pliable. Pour the thyme leaves over the dough, drizzle the remaining olive oil and salt, and incorporate the leaves into the dough with your hands. Cover the bowl with a damp cloth and put it in a dark draft-free place to rise for 1½ hours.

Preheat the oven to 400°F. Roll out the dough to a 1-inch thickness on an oiled surface and cut with any desired cookie cutter (I like to use a star shape). Brush each star with olive oil and bake for 15 minutes until golden brown. They are best hot out of the oven. Freeze any extras.

mezze

"Eating the mezze way" is often the way I like to entertain. It is relaxing and casual.
It also does not have to be lavish. It can be as simple as a bowl of olives, labneh,
vegetable crudités and fresh bread. As long as you have a variety of tastes and textures,
you have it right!

Mezze comes from the Persian word maza meaning "to taste or savor." The people of the
Mediterranean share a lot, and the tradition of eating small portions of many foods leisurely
with guests is one that has stood the test of time.

I like my mezze spread to be a feast for the eyes. The colorful plates should tempt you to
indulge. With such dishes as flaky pastries with lemony spinach filling, baba ghanouj
glistening with ruby red pomegranate seeds, succulent sausages doused with a tart
pomegranate molasses, and tabbouleh with the fresh smell of herbs, you are spoiled for choice.

In some countries this salad is known as baba ghanouj. (For the baba ghanouj dip, see page 42.)
Salatet al raheb is another name for this famous and nutritious salad. It has a medley of textures and the classic sour
and sweet tastes that are characteristic of so many Middle Eastern dishes. Every time I have a barbecue I make this salad.
It is quite a chameleon, as it adapts to any grilled meat. It's a salad, a salsa and a dip – all in one. I even serve it as a topping for crostini.

Baba Ghanouj Salad

4–6 servings

4 medium eggplants • 4 green onions, sliced thin (whites only)
1 shallot, finely chopped • 3 cloves garlic, mashed
juice of 1 lemon (or more) • sea salt • 20 cherry tomatoes, seeded and sliced in quarters
¼ cup parsley, finely chopped • ¼ cup fresh mint, finely chopped
½ cup walnuts, toasted and coarsely chopped
handful of fresh pomegranate seeds, to garnish • pomegranate molasses • extra virgin olive oil

Pierce the eggplants all over with a fork and place them on a charcoal or gas grill over medium heat (or broil it in the oven). Keep turning them evenly to char the skin. It will blacken and begin to collapse after 25–30 minutes. Remove and place in a colander or on a rack to drain some of the juices. When cool enough, slice in half lengthwise. Peel away the charred skin and place in a colander to drain further.

Chop the eggplant into small chunks and place in a bowl. Add the green onions, shallot, garlic, lemon juice and salt. Lastly, add the tomatoes and toss gently, taking care not to mash the eggplant. Sprinkle on the parsely and mint. Spoon into small serving plates, then scatter the walnuts on top, garnish with the pomegranate seeds and drizzle a little pomegranate molasses on top. Drizzle on the olive oil and serve immediately.

Roasting the beets brings out their natural sweetness. I like to accentuate their color by adding purslane leaves and slivers of orange rind.

■■■■■■■■■■■■■■■■■■■■■■■■■■■■■■■■■■■■■■

Beet and Purslane Salad with Citrus Dressing

4–6 servings

6 medium beets • olive oil for roasting beets • ¼ cup red vinegar • juice and zest of ½ orange
1 garlic clove, mashed • 1 Tbsp sugar • sea salt
¼ cup extra virgin olive oil • 1 large handful of purslane (leaves only) (watercress or arugula are good substitutes)
slivers of orange zest, to garnish

Preheat oven to 400°F. Wash the beets, removing the stalks if necessary, and dry well. Rub them all over with olive oil and wrap each beet individually with foil. Place on a baking pan and roast for approximately 1½ hours. Remove and unwrap. Cool completely. Peel the beets and slice into wedges (gloves are recommended here). Set aside to prepare the dressing.

To make the dressing, place the vinegar, orange juice and zest, garlic, sugar, salt and olive oil into a bowl and whisk together well. When ready to serve, place the beets in individual small plates or one big platter. Scatter on top the purslane leaves. Drizzle the dressing all over the salad. Garnish with slivers of orange zest. Serve immediately.

*"Where's the hummus?" was one of the first phrases my dear nephew Gabe learned when he was only two years old.
My friends ask the same question too, and want the recipe and the secret behind this divine dip. I believe that the simplest of dishes
can be the trickiest to make. Hummus is composed of few ingredients, but it is the delicate balance of each that creates the best results.
The ultimate hummus is attainable if you soak the dried chickpeas overnight and cook them the following day. Removing the skins
also ensures a creamier hummus. And, of course, there is no substitute for fresh garlic, fresh lemon juice and good quality tahini
(pure ground sesame paste). I sometimes sauté finely diced lamb, seasoned with cinnamon and allspice,
and serve it on top of the plated hummus for a delicious variation.*

Hummus

4-6 servings

**1 cup dried chickpeas, soaked overnight in lots of cold water with 1 Tbsp baking soda
½ cup ice cubes • ¼ cup tahini • 2 cloves garlic • ¼ cup yogurt • ¼ cup lemon juice • sea salt
extra virgin olive oil • paprika or cayenne pepper, to garnish**

After soaking the chickpeas overnight, discard the soaking water and replace with new cold water. Place the chickpeas with the water in a saucepan over medium to medium-high heat and bring to a boil. Skim off the foam that comes to the surface. Lower the heat to a simmer and cook the chickpeas until tender, for approximately 1 hour. When cool enough to handle, rub off as many skins as you can. Using a slotted spoon, remove ½ cup of cooked chickpeas for garnish. Scoop out the remaining chickpeas and place them in a food processor.

Start the machine and add the ice cubes, tahini, garlic, yogurt and lemon juice. (The ice cools the hummus, helps break down the chickpeas and makes the hummus creamy.) Add the salt and taste, adjusting by adding more lemon if you like. The mixture should be creamy and a little runny. It will thicken when you put it in the fridge until it is ready to serve. Spread the hummus onto small, shallow plates and use a spoon to make a deep groove. Drizzle on the olive oil. Garnish with the reserved chickpeas and a sprinkle of paprika. Serve with fresh, warm pita bread and plenty of vegetables for dipping.

While this roasted cauliflower dish is good hot, I like it best the day after, cold from the fridge and rolled up in a soft pita bread. On a hot summer day, it's a nice cool side dish to have with grilled meat. And for me, a mezze table wouldn't be complete without it. My mother used to make this all the time and wouldn't dream of adding orange juice and zest – that's my thing. I like the sweet citrus flavors of orange. It balances and cuts through the earthy tahini. M'hammara (Roasted Red Pepper Dip) is a must on the mezze table. Roasting the peppers brings out their sweetness along with a subtle smokiness. I sometimes mix in a couple tablespoons of labneh (the thickened yogurt dip – see page 25) to create a variation on this dip that is both sweet and tart.

Roasted Cauliflower with Citrus Tahini Sauce

4 servings

1 head of cauliflower • ¼ cup olive oil • sea salt
juice of 2 lemons • zest and juice of ½ orange
(save some zest to garnish) • 1 cup water • ¾ cup tahini
3 Tbsp olive oil • 2 cloves garlic, mashed • 2 medium onions,
sliced thin • ½ cup toasted pine nuts, to garnish
¼ cup slivered pistachios, to garnish

Preheat the oven to 425°F. Take the whole head of cauliflower and cut (core included) into 4 thick slices. Place on a large baking sheet, coat with oil and season with salt. Roast until golden and crisp and cooked through. Turn over halfway being careful not to break the cauliflower. It should take about 20 minutes. Mix the lemon juice, orange juice and zest, water and tahini to make a creamy sauce and leave aside.

In a deep frying pan, heat the 3 Tbsp olive oil and sauté the onions and garlic until light golden and soft. Pour the tahini sauce over the cooked onions and bring to a simmer until the flavors mingle and it thickens slightly. Taste to adjust seasonings. Serve drizzled over the roasted cauliflower and garnish with toasted pine nuts, slivered pistachios and orange zest.

Roasted Red Pepper Dip (M'hammara)

4–6 servings

4 large red peppers
4 hot red chilies, seeded and chopped
½ cup toasted walnuts, coarsely chopped
½ cup toasted pine nuts • 2 cloves garlic, mashed
juice of 1 lemon • 2 Tbsp pomegranate molasses
1 cup fresh bread crumbs (made with white toasted
bread, crust removed)
1 tsp sugar • sea salt • ¼ cup olive oil
toasted walnuts, to garnish • extra virgin olive oil

On a barbecue grill, roast the red peppers enough to char the skin. (Alternatively, broil the peppers in the oven.) Remove the peppers from the heat, put them into a glass bowl and cover with plastic wrap. When fully cooled, peel the charred skin, remove the seeds and membrane and chop into chunks. Lastly, put the peppers along with the remaining ingredients (except the olive oil) into a food processor and pulse to a coarse consistency. Pour in the ¼ cup olive oil while the motor is still running in a slow, steady stream until the mixture comes together but not liquid. Eat as a dip or as a topping on toasted crostini, garnished with toasted walnuts and a drizzle of extra virgin olive oil.

Tahini is the perfect partner for fish. It is creamy and nutty. The onions add a welcome sweetness to the tahini sauce, the lemon juice cuts through the richness of it and the orange juice and zest take it entirely to another level. My mother is baffled by this last addition and shakes her head, not too pleased about me changing her recipe. I tread carefully at this point and serve her a piece with an extra squeeze of lemon. After two bites even my toughest critic becomes a fan. Whew!

Poached Fish in Tahini Sauce with Crispy Onions

6 servings

½ cup tahini • 3 cloves garlic, mashed • juice of 2 lemons • juice of 1 orange
zest of ½ orange • 1 cup water • sea salt • 6 Tbsp olive oil
6 pieces of white fish fillets (sea bass, halibut, cod)
2 small onions, thinly sliced • ¼ cup toasted pine nuts, to garnish

Make the sauce by combining the tahini with the garlic, lemon juice and orange juice and zest. The mixture will seize at first; but gradually add the water and it will begin to soften. Add the salt and mix well to achieve a runny, creamy sauce. Set aside.

In a large frying pan, heat 3 Tbsp of the olive oil and place the fish fillet skin side down to crisp up for about 3 minutes. Turn over to brown on the other side for 2 minutes. Remove and set aside (it will finish cooking in the sauce).

In another large frying pan heat the remaining 3 Tbsp of olive oil and fry the onions until golden and crisp but not burned. Remove and place on absorbent paper towel.

Using the same frying pan pour in the tahini-citrus mixture. Stir and season with salt. Reserve some onions for garnish and add the rest to the sauce. Allow the sauce to come to a boil for 2 minutes. Lower the heat and slide the fish in the tahini sauce. Swirl around to coat the fish evenly. Leave undisturbed for 5 minutes to finish poaching the fish. Serve hot in little plates garnished with toasted pine nuts and the reserved crispy onions.

Summer in Canada was often hot and humid. Even though it was a short season, we made sure we ate watermelon daily. The cold sweetness of the watermelon contrasts with the saltiness of the white cheese. The mint adds color and freshness. And the rosewater? Simply exotic …

Exotic Watermelon and Cheese Salad

4–6 servings

5 cups watermelon • 2 cups feta cheese or halloumi
1 handful fresh mint leaves • rosewater in a spritzer

Cut the watermelon into bite-sized cubes or triangles and keep cool and covered in the fridge. Cut the cheese in a similar shape and set aside.

When you're ready to serve, place a few pieces of watermelon on a plate. Add a few pieces of cheese. Scatter a few fresh mint leaves. I keep some rosewater in a pump spritzer. Spray a light mist of rosewater on the salad and serve immediately.

This is a heavenly combination.

This is the second-most popular dish (next to hummus). The smoky taste of the chargrilled eggplant sets it apart. It is a great dip as part of a mezze spread or a side dish for barbecued meats or fish. This dip is known by two names, one being baba ghanouj and the other mutabbal beitinjan. Whatever you decide to call it, everyone eating it will agree it is delicious.

Mutabbal Beitinjan

4-6 servings

4 medium eggplants • ¼ cup tahini • ½ cup yogurt
2 cloves garlic, mashed • juice of 1 lemon (maybe more)
sea salt • extra virgin olive oil • fresh pomegranate seeds, to garnish
¼ cup toasted pine nuts

Pierce the eggplants all over with a fork and place them on a charcoal or gas grill over medium heat (or broil it in the oven). Keep turning them to evenly char the skin. The eggplants will begin to collapse after 25–30 minutes. Remove them at this point and place in a colander or on a rack to allow some of the juices to drain. When cool enough to handle, slice in half lengthwise, scoop out the flesh and place in a colander to continue to drain further.

Place the eggplant in a bowl and mash with a fork or a potato masher, making sure not to overmash since you want to keep some texture. Add the tahini, yogurt and garlic and mix well. Gradually pour in the lemon juice and salt and keep tasting to adjust, if necessary. Scoop the mixture into small decorative plates. One option is to spread the mixture almost to the edge of the plate. Drizzle with extra virgin olive oil and garnish with the fresh pomegranate seeds and pine nuts.

I've never visited Syria but I have heard of the breathtaking beauty of cherry trees laden with blossoms in the spring. Many dishes using cherries in season were born in the historic city of Aleppo. Combining sweet and sour fruit with meat dates back to medieval times in the Arab world. It lives on to this day in many dishes. I like to make these little meatballs as part of the mezze table for an unexpected taste combination. Of course use fresh cherries when in season, but dried cherries are also delicious.

Kofta (Meatballs with Sweet and Sour Cherry Sauce)

8-10 servings

Cherry Sauce
2 cups fresh cherries or 1 cup dried cherries • ¼ cup honey • juice of 1 lemon
½ cup water • 1 tsp cinnamon • 2 Tbsp olive oil • 1 shallot, chopped
1 clove garlic, minced • ½ cup fresh mint, chopped

Meatballs
1 lb ground lamb • ½ cup sparkling water • 4 cloves garlic, minced
¼ cup fresh cilantro, chopped • ½ tsp cloves • ½ tsp cinnamon
½ tsp cumin • ½ tsp allspice • salt and pepper • 3 Tbsp olive oil

½ cup pine nuts, toasted, to garnish • ½ cup fresh pomegranate seeds, to garnish

Start by making the cherry sauce, which you can leave aside while you make the meatballs.

In a small saucepan combine the cherries, honey, lemon juice, water and cinnamon and heat to boil. Lower heat and allow to simmer for 5 minutes. Set aside. In another saucepan, heat the olive oil and sauté the shallot and garlic. Pour in the hot cherry mixture and cook on medium heat until tender and slightly thickened. Add salt and pepper to taste. Lastly, stir in the mint.

In a bowl place the ground lamb, sparkling water, garlic, cilantro, cloves, cinnamon, cumin, allspice, salt and pepper. Mix lightly to incorporate all the ingredients and shape into small meatballs. Set aside until ready to cook. When the sauce is ready, heat 3 Tbsp olive oil in a large frying pan. Place a few meatballs to fry and brown all over. Remove and keep warm until all are ready to serve. Serve hot and drizzle the cherry sauce over the meatballs and garnish with the pine nuts and fresh pomegranate seeds.

Tabbouleh is the quintessential salad of Lebanon and my absolute favorite. It's a simple salad with few ingredients, and supermarket creations don't compare to the homemade version. Parsley and tomato are the main ingredients. It should be fresh, crisp and lemony. Tartare is one of the ingenious dishes that make precious meat go a little further. The Japanese have their sushi, the French have their steak tartare and the Arabs have their kibbeh nayye. Whenever raw meat is eaten, know your source and choose organic and the freshest and leanest fillet to be eaten on the same day. The bulgur gives it texture, and the rose petals add a nice flavor and color. (Rose petals are an ancient ingredient used in many Middle Eastern dishes – they are sometimes candied and used to decorate various sweets. Omit them if you cannot find them.) Have plenty of mint, onions and fresh pita bread to eat with every bite and use the best fruity olive oil.

Tabbouleh

4–6 servings

½ cup fine bulgur • 6 firm ripe tomatoes
4 large bunches flat-leaf parsley, stalks removed
4 green onions, trimmed (whites only)
1 handful fresh mint leaves, stalks removed
juice of 2 lemons (or less) • ½ tsp ground cinnamon
½ tsp ground allspice • ½ cup extra virgin olive oil
1 tsp freshly ground black pepper • sea salt

Rinse the bulgur in cold water, squeeze out the excess water and place in a bowl. Finely dice the tomatoes while keeping their shape and place on top of the bulgur. The juice from the tomatoes will soften the bulgur, and the bulgur will soak up the flavor. Wash the parsley and drain well. Use a salad spinner to get rid of as much excess water as possible to ensure the tabbouleh will be crisp and not soggy.

Grab hold of a big bunch of parsley and, gathering tightly, use the sharpest knife to chop the leaves thinly and finely (don't use a food processor). Slice the green onions and mint in the same way to attain the same texture. Place the chopped parsley, green onions and mint in a big bowl. Add the tomatoes and bulgur. Pour the lemon juice on top with the spices, then drizzle over the olive oil, salt and pepper. The best way to mix this salad is to use your hands to gently toss and coat every leaf evenly. The vegetables and herbs can be chopped in advance, but wait until the last minute to mix everything. Serve immediately with grilled fish, meat or chicken. For an elegant presentation, try serving tabbouleh in small baby lettuce leaves or mini cabbage leaves.

Kibbeh Tartare

4–6 servings

½ cup fine bulgur • ¾ cup cold water
½ onion, sliced fine • ½ tsp allspice
1 tsp cinnamon • 1 tsp cumin
1 tsp dried marjoram • 1 tsp dried rose petals (optional)
1 hot red chili, seeded and chopped
6 basil leaves • salt and pepper
10 oz leanest lamb, from the leg,
finely ground (or beef tenderloin)
extra virgin olive oil • fresh mint leaves, to garnish

Soak the bulgur in just enough cold water to slightly cover, for about 5 minutes. Drain and squeeze out all of the water and place in a bowl. In a food processor (or a large mortar and pestle) put the onion, spices, rose petals, chili and basil and pulse (or crush) to make a paste. Pour this into the bulgur and season with salt and pepper.

Just before serving have a bowl of ice-cold water beside you. Begin to incorporate the bulgur into the meat, wetting your hands a couple of times to help the mixture come together. The result should be smooth. Spoon and spread into small shallow plates. Use a teaspoon to make a decorative rim and drizzle on the extra virgin olive oil. Garnish with mint leaves. Serve as part of a mezze spread with plenty of pita bread, more fresh mint, and some sweet red onions.

Next to tabbouleh, fried kibbeh is the second-most popular dish in Lebanon and Syria particularly. Delicious fragrant stuffing is encased within a crisp shell of bulgur, meat and spices. Versions of kibbeh can be made with potato, pumpkin and even fish. When I make kibbeh I always make a big batch and freeze the extras. On days when I don't know what to cook I pull out my frozen kibbeh and make a salad. A big bowl of yogurt and olives are always on my table. Voilà, instant lunch!

Fried Kibbeh

Makes 24 kibbeh

Filling

¼ cup olive oil • ½ cup pine nuts
2 medium onions, finely chopped
½ lb lean lamb, finely ground • 1 tsp cinnamon
1 tsp sumac • 1 tsp allspice • salt and pepper

Kibbeh Dough

1 onion, finely chopped • 1 tsp cinnamon • 1 tsp cumin
1 tsp allspice • 1 tsp marjoram
¼ cup dried rose petals (optional)
2 cups fine bulgur, presoaked in cold water
1 lb lean lamb, finely ground twice
olive oil for deep-frying

First prepare the filling. In a large frying pan heat the oil and sauté the pine nuts until lightly golden. Remove with a slotted spoon and set aside. Add the onions to the same oil and sauté until soft and translucent. Add the ground lamb and continue to stir to cook through. Season with the cinnamon, sumac, allspice, salt and pepper. Add the pine nuts. Taste to adjust seasonings. Set aside to cool.

To make the kibbeh dough, in a food processor purée the onion with the spices and rose petals or pound them to a paste using a big mortar and pestle. Place in a large bowl. Squeeze out every drop of water from the bulgur (I place the bulgur in a tea towel to absorb most of the moisture). Add the bulgur to the spicy paste and mix well. Add the meat and work it in to make it all come together. A couple of tablespoons of cold water will help the dough to become smooth and easy to mold.

Moisten hands with a little water, take a portion of kibbeh dough roughly the size of a golf ball. Form into a uniform ball. Make an indent in the center of the ball, cupping it in your palm. Using your thumb, enlarge the indent, making sure to keep turning the dough to make the shell as evenly thin as possible. Fill the shell with the cooled filling. Close it and smooth it out to enclose completely. Form the kibbeh into the traditional pointed-oblong (this is tricky at first, but with practice you'll be a pro). Continue until all are formed. At this point you can freeze any extras in a freezerproof container.

In a deep heavy-bottomed saucepan, heat the olive oil to 350°F. Fry the kibbeh balls until golden brown on all sides. Serve hot with cucumber and yogurt mint salad.

Cucumber and Yogurt Mint Salad

4-6 servings

2 cloves garlic • 2 cups plain yogurt • sea salt
4 Lebanese or Japanese cucumbers, seeded, thinly sliced
handful of fresh mint, finely chopped • 1 Tbsp dried mint

In a mortar and pestle pound the garlic to a soft paste. Place in a bowl, add the yogurt and mix well. Add salt to taste. Just before serving, tumble in the cucumbers and fold in gently. Sprinkle in the fresh and dried mint. Serve with the kibbeh.

This is a beautiful vegetarian dish best eaten at room temperature or even cold straight from the fridge. It makes a perfect side dish with rice or meat. Traditionally it is eaten like many mezze dishes by pinching morsels with pita bread. The braised whole garlic is a sweet surprise.

Braised Green Beans and Tomatoes

4-6 servings

½ cup olive oil • 12 cloves garlic, sliced thin
2 onions, chopped • 4 cups green beans, cut diagonally
4 cups chopped tomatoes • 1 head of garlic, cloves separated, unpeeled
2 Tbsp tomato paste • 1 Tbsp sugar • salt and pepper

In a large frying pan, heat the olive oil and sauté garlic and onions until soft. Add the green beans and stir well (beans will turn a deep green). Cover and continue cooking for 5 minutes.

Remove lid and add chopped tomatoes, cloves of unpeeled garlic, tomato paste and sugar. Season with salt and pepper. Lower heat, cover, and allow to simmer for 30 minutes until sauce thickens and beans are tender.

At a mezze table you are spoiled for choice and these herb and nut–crusted labneh balls fit right in. They're creamy, crunchy and savory all in one bite. Part of the joy of eating this way is having a chance to taste a variety of diverse flavors. These balls make a delicious spread on toast for breakfast as well. Make sure to allow two days to prepare the labneh. Store any extra dry dukkah mixture (don't store with the fresh thyme) in a sealed jar in the fridge. It will keep for a long time.

Herb and Nut–Crusted Labneh Balls

Makes 25 balls

Labneh
for recipe see page 181

Dukkah
½ cup sesame seeds • ½ cup hazelnuts
½ cup toasted pistachios, chopped • 3 Tbsp cumin seeds
1 tsp sumac • 1 tsp dried chili flakes
½ cup za'atar • sea salt flakes
black pepper, coarsely ground • ½ handful fresh thyme, stems removed, finely chopped

To make the dukkah mixture, toast the sesame seeds in a dry frying pan stirring continuously. Remove and set aside to cool. Toast the hazelnuts in the oven and rub the skins while they're hot in a tea towel. Chop or grind the nuts but not too finely. Pound the cumin seeds with a mortar and pestle. Mix all the spices and nuts as well as the salt and pepper and set aside. Leave out the fresh thyme to be added only before you serve.

To make the labneh, see page 181. When it's ready, remove the very thick labneh from the cloth and roll out golf-ball-sized portions in your hands. It will have the consistency of goat cheese. It helps to oil your hands first. Roll the balls around in some of the spice/nut mixture and sprinkle on the fresh thyme. To store any extra labneh balls without the dukkah mixture, place in a clean sterilized jar and pour in enough extra virgin olive oil to completely immerse them. Keep refrigerated for up to 1 week. Serve with the toasted pita wedges (see recipe on page 9) or crostini, alongside tomato slices, fresh mint and/or arugula leaves.

Bamia bil zeit is the Arabic name for this lovely dish. Bil zeit means "in oil" and implies that the dish is vegetarian and can be eaten cold. I prefer to use baby okra, which has fewer seeds. Many vegetables like zucchini, green beans, broad beans, spinach and Swiss chard can be made the same way, with or without the tomatoes. Have plenty of pita bread to use to pinch and grab morsels of the bamia. It also makes a great vegetable side dish, hot or cold, next to grilled lamb or chicken.

Baby Okra and Sautéed Tomatoes

4 servings

10 cloves garlic, finely sliced • ¼ cup extra virgin olive oil
1 pkg (14 oz) frozen baby okra • 6 tomatoes, chopped
1 head of garlic, cloves separated, unpeeled
1 tsp cinnamon • ½ tsp allspice
2 Tbsp sugar • salt and pepper

Quickly rinse the frozen okra in cold water to get rid of any ice crystals. Place a large frying pan on medium heat and sauté the garlic with the olive oil until soft. Add the okra and sauté together for 5 minutes. Pour in the chopped tomatoes and the unpeeled garlic cloves. Stir gently, being careful not to break the okra. Season with cinnamon, allspice, sugar, and salt and pepper. Reduce to a simmer.

Cover and leave to cook to develop the flavors for 10–15 minutes. The tomatoes will release their juice, to make a sauce. The okra will also release some of its juice, which will help thicken the sauce. Turn off the heat and allow to cool completely. Serve cold or room temperature. It tastes even better the next day.

Filled pastries are a delicacy and a staple in Arabic cuisine. Food historians trace back the origin of empanadas to the meat-filled pies of Arabia of long ago. The choice of fillings is endless. When I'm in the mood I'll make a big batch of the dough, fill them and freeze the extras. They can be fried frozen and are a nice addition when you want to entertain the mezze way.

Sambousek Two Ways

Makes approx. 60 turnovers

Dough
4 cups flour • 1 Tbsp baking powder • 1 tsp salt • ½ cup oil • 1½ cups lukewarm water

Lamb Filling
2 Tbsp olive oil • 1 onion, finely chopped • 3 cloves garlic, minced • 1 lb very lean ground lamb
1 tsp allspice • 1 tsp cinnamon • 3 Tbsp fresh mint, finely chopped • 2 Tbsp pomegranate molasses
2 Tbsp sumac • salt and pepper • ½ cup toasted pine nuts

Cheese Filling
13 oz feta cheese • 7 oz mozzarella cheese, shredded • 1 egg white • 1–2 Tbsp fresh thyme or oregano

peanut oil for deep-frying

In a large bowl pour in the flour, baking powder and salt. Make a well in the center and add the oil and water. Using your hands, combine to make a soft dough. Knead for 2 minutes on a working surface until smooth. Divide and form into small equal-sized balls the size of a walnut and place on a tray. Cover with plastic wrap and leave to rest while you prepare the filling.

To make the lamb filling, heat the oil in a large frying pan and sauté the onion and the garlic until soft. Add the meat and brown while stirring. Add the spices, herbs, pomegranate molasses, sumac, salt, pepper and pine nuts. Taste to adjust the seasonings. Place in a colander to drain any excess oil. Cool completely before using as a filling for the sambousek.

To make the cheese filling, in a bowl mix the feta cheese, mozzarella, egg white and thyme.

Take a ball of dough and flatten into a small disk by hand or rolling pin. Place a teaspoonful of the cheese filling in the center. Fold over and press the edges together to make a crescent. Pick up the filled crescent, and fold and twist to crimp the edges and give it a finished look. For the triangle shape, start with the same round disk. Place the filling in t he center and gather the corners to meet in the center to make a triangle. Pinch to seal the three borders. At this point you can freeze the filled sambousek for later use. In a heavy-bottomed saucepan, heat the oil to 350°F and fry 4 or 5 sambousek at a time until golden brown and crisp, about 1 minute on each side. Serve hot.

A change from tempura batter. Use the versatile knafe (also spelled kataife) pastry, a fine, vermicelli-like pastry, for this savory snack. It also makes a perfect lunch with a salad and a spicy dip on the side (like dakkous; see recipe on page 89). The citrus nutty center is a lovely surprise inside the sweet prawn. These prawns are seriously crunchy. You could bake them but they taste better fried.

Citrus and Almond Prawns Wrapped in Knafe Pastry

4 servings

1 pkg (1 lb) knafe dough, defrosted • 1 cup toasted flaked almonds
zest of 1 lemon • zest of 1 orange • zest of 1 lime • salt and pepper
20 medium fresh prawns, shelled, cleaned and butterflied with tails intact
salt and pepper • peanut oil for deep-frying

Spread the knafe dough on a working surface and cover with a damp cloth. In a small bowl, mix the almonds with the lemon, orange and lime zests. Season the prawn with salt and pepper and open the backs. Take a pinch of the almond mixture and place in the open area of the prawn. Close together to encase the filling and continue until all prawns are filled.

Take a few strands of the knafe pastry dough, lay them down flat and spread away from you. Place a filled prawn at the end closest to you and roll the dough around the prawn, ensuring the filling does not come out. Leave the tails exposed. It will look like a cocoon. Proceed to wrap all the prawns in the same way. Keep covered until ready to fry.

Heat the oil in a heavy-bottomed saucepan to 350°F. Using tongs, gently lower the wrapped prawn in the hot oil, one at a time. Don't let go of the rolled prawn with the tongs in the oil until it holds together. Fry about 5 at a time until golden and crisp. Remove and place on absorbent paper. Serve immediately.

I love to add these chicken wings as a hot option on my mezze table. The spices and herbs I use make them exotic and very tasty. Ten of my children's cousins came over one evening. They are all teenagers and wings connoisseurs. I must have made over a hundred of these wings along with a huge batch of banadoora maklia (hot tomato salsa). In the blink of an eye they were gone. I guess they were that good.

Spicy Chicken Wings with Fresh Hot Tomato Salsa

4 servings

20 chicken wings (tips removed) • 4 cloves garlic, minced
¼ cup fresh cilantro, chopped • ¼ cup olive oil • ½ tsp cinnamon • 1 tsp smoked paprika
1 tsp cayenne pepper • ¼ cup honey • juice of 1 lemon
3 Tbsp pomegranate molasses • salt and pepper

Hot Tomato Salsa
¼ cup olive oil • 8 hot red or green chilies, sliced to reveal seeds
8 tomatoes, coarsely chopped • sea salt

Make a marinade with all of the ingredients in a large bowl and toss in the chicken wings. Leave aside to absorb the flavors for 1 hour in the fridge. Preheat the oven to 350°F. Place the wings spread apart on a shallow roasting pan. Bake until crisp and cooked on the inside, about 35 minutes. Serve hot with spicy tomato salsa.

To make the salsa, heat the olive oil in a large frying pan and add the chilies, browning them slightly. Tumble in the chopped tomatoes. Season with salt and bring to a boil. Lower the heat and cover for 15 minutes to release the juices and allow the tomatoes to stew. Uncover and allow the liquid to reduce and thicken slightly. Remove and cool. Best eaten at room temperature. Good as a dipping sauce for these wings or for dipping fresh warm pita bread. Warning: this salsa will bring tears to your eyes!

One of my favorite cheeses is halloumi. It is salty and lends itself to so many ways of cooking. Here I fry the cubes of cheese and put them in the salad just before I serve it. The saltiness and crisp crust of the halloumi goes so well with the sweet grapes, salty olives and the bite of the herbs. The pomegranate dressing pulls it all together.

Green Salad with Fried Halloumi, Grapes and Pomegranate Dressing

4 servings

2 large handfuls of green and red lettuce leaves • 1 handful purslane leaves (watercress or arugula are good substitutes)
1 handful fresh wild thyme (or fresh oregano) • ½ cup green seedless grapes (cut in half)
½ cup red seedless grapes (cut in half) • ½ cup pitted green olives
1 lb halloumi cheese • flour • 2 Tbsp clarified butter
½ cup fresh pomegranate seeds • fresh mint

Dressing
3 cloves garlic, mashed • juice and zest of 1 lemon • juice and zest of ½ orange
1 Tbsp sugar • 2 Tbsp pomegranate molasses
¼ cup extra virgin olive oil

Make the dressing by combining the garlic, lemon and orange juice, zest, sugar and pomegranate molasses. Whisk in the olive oil and set aside.

Place the lettuce leaves, purslane and fresh thyme on a nice serving plate. Scatter the grapes and olives on the leaves.

Cut the halloumi into bite-sized cubes and blot with a paper towel to remove the excess water. Dredge the cubes in some flour.

In a large frying pan, heat the clarified butter and fry the cheese cubes until golden all over. Remove and place in the salad. Drizzle the dressing on top and toss gently. Garnish with the fresh pomegranate seeds and mint and serve immediately.

This is a classic vegetarian mezze dish. Sometimes it is called yolangee. Essentially the filling is similar to tabbouleh but using rice instead of cracked wheat (bulgur). You can make this dish a day ahead and keep it refrigerated. Cook the following day and keep at room temperature until you are ready to serve it. A couple of stuffed vine leaves on top of a garden salad make a light and tasty lunch.

Lemony Braised Stuffed Vine Leaves with Mini Zucchini

8–10 servings

2 potatoes • 5 cups fresh parsley, chopped • 1 cup fresh mint, chopped
15 medium tomatoes, diced • 8 green onions, chopped • juice of 4 lemons
½ cup olive oil • 1 tsp cinnamon • 1 tsp allspice • salt and pepper
2 cups short-grain white rice, presoaked, drained • 1 cup water
12 small zucchini, washed, scrubbed, cored (see instructions on page 115)
1 jar (1 lb) grapevine leaves, washed, drained and stalks removed

Peel and slice the potatoes into ¼-inch-thick rounds. Place them in water to keep from discoloring.

In a large bowl, place parsley, mint, tomatoes and green onions. Add the lemon juice and oil and season with spices, salt and pepper. Taste and adjust the seasonings. It should be tangy and juicy. Stir in the rice and combine well.

Begin by stuffing the zucchini with the rice-vegetable mixture and set them aside. Fill the vine leaves. Reserve the dressing that is left over from the rice-vegetable mixture as that will be used as the cooking liquid. If you have extra vine leaves after using up all the filling, you can freeze them in a plastic bag.

In a 6-quart pot, place the sliced potatoes in an even layer on the bottom. Place the zucchini on top of the potatoes, tightly side by side radiating out from the center. For the second layer, place the stuffed vine leaves on top, seam side down, with their short ends touching the edge of the pot, forming a circle. Work toward the center. Pour the remaining dressing over everything and add the cup of water to the pot. Place a heatproof plate smaller than the diameter of the pot on top to ensure everything stays in place.

Place on a medium to medium-high heat and allow to come to a boil. Lower heat to minimum, cover and allow to simmer for 1½ hours. Keep a watchful eye that there is enough liquid while they are cooking. When done the vine leaves should be meltingly soft and cooked throughout. Remove from the heat and leave to cool completely before flipping onto a serving platter. Best eaten at room temperature.

How to stuff vine leaves: *Take one vine leaf (or half a vine leaf) and place it on your work surface, shiny side down. Using your fingers, pick up about a teaspoonful or less of the filling for the meat version on page 139 (be more generous with the vegetarian version above) and place near the top of the end nearest to you. Roll forward to cover the filling and fold over the two sides to the center and roll away from you. Use a firm hand to ensure the filling is completely enclosed. Continue until all of the leaves are filled and set aside. They will look like little cigars.*

Moussaqa'a in Arabic means "cold." This is how it is best eaten. It is made with a little olive oil and is totally vegetarian. In Turkey and Greece there are also tasty versions of this dish. This is my take on this classic. It is so simple to prepare. Both the sauce and the eggplants can be prepared ahead of time and assembled in minutes.

▪ ▪

Moussaqa'a

12 servings

3 large eggplants • ¼ cup olive oil and peanut oil mixture
2 Tbsp olive oil • 1 onion, chopped fine
6 cloves of garlic, sliced thin • 12 tomatoes, diced
1 tsp allspice • 1 tsp cinnamon
2 Tbsp sugar • 1 Tbsp pomegranate molasses
salt and pepper • about ¾ cup cooked chickpeas, rinsed and drained if canned
½ cup pine nuts, toasted • ½ cup chopped fresh mint

Preheat the oven to 450°F. Peel the eggplants and cut lengthwise (about ½ inch thick). Brush both sides with the oil mixture and place on a baking sheet. Roast until golden brown, about 15 minutes in total, flipping them over halfway. Remove to cool completely.

In a large frying pan, heat 2 Tbsp of olive oil. Add the onion and garlic and sauté until soft and translucent. Add the diced tomatoes, allspice, cinnamon, sugar, pomegranate molasses, salt and pepper. Allow to come to a boil. Add the drained chickpeas to the tomato sauce. Lower the heat and leave to simmer and thicken slightly (about 5 minutes). Lastly, stir in half the amount of pine nuts and set aside.

To serve, put one slice of roasted eggplant on a platter, spoon the tomato chickpea sauce over the thicker side and fold over to cover the filling. Proceed with the other slices. Garnish with mint and the remaining toasted pine nuts. Serve with a salad. Moussaqa'a can also be a great side dish with any grilled meat.

I have made a few changes to this traditional salad. To bring out their sweetness, I roast the beets instead of boiling them.
I like to finely dice them for a prettier presentation. It's a good idea to toss in the dressing at the last minute before serving.

Shamandar (Beet) Dip

4–6 servings

6 medium beets • olive oil • ¼ cup yogurt • 2 cloves garlic, mashed
2 Tbsp tahini • pinch of cumin • juice and zest of 1 lemon
juice and zest of ½ orange • sea salt • extra virgin olive oil
fresh mint leaves, to garnish

Heat the oven to 400°F. Wash, dry and coat each beet with olive oil. Wrap each one individually with foil or parchment and place on a baking sheet. Roast for approximately 1½ hours until they are cooked through. Remove from the oven and cool completely. Put on some gloves. Peel the cooked beets, dice finely and place in a bowl.

Mix the yogurt, garlic, tahini, cumin, lemon juice and zest, orange juice and zest and salt to make a dressing. Pour over the chopped beets and fold to combine well. Place in small shallow dishes, drizzle on extra virgin olive oil and garnish with mint leaves.

This same spinach filling can be made and used to fill a traditional bread dough. They would be equally as delicious. Here I have used filo pastry, which bakes crispy and light. The sumac adds a lemony tartness to the earthy spinach and accentuates the sweet onions. These are totally addictive. I dare you to eat just one!

Spinach-Filled Filo Triangles

Makes 24 triangles

5 cups fresh spinach, washed and drained • ¼ cup olive oil
1 medium red onion, finely chopped • 2 green onions, finely chopped (whites only)
juice of 1 lemon • salt and pepper • 1 Tbsp sumac • 1 tsp ground nutmeg
½ cup pine nuts • 12 sheets filo dough, defrosted
½ cup melted butter and ¼ cup olive oil, mixed

Remove the stalks on the spinach leaves, cut the leaves into thin slices and set aside in a large bowl. In a large frying pan, heat the olive oil and sauté the chopped onions until soft. Remove the pan from heat, stir in the spinach, green onions, lemon juice, salt, pepper, sumac and nutmeg. The spinach will begin to wilt and release its liquid. Tip everything into a colander to drain. Mix in the pine nuts. Taste to adjust the seasonings and leave aside to prepare the dough.

Preheat the oven to 375°F. Cut the filo sheets in half lengthwise. Use one sheet at a time and cover the rest to keep it from drying out. Brush the sheet with the butter and oil combination and fold it over lengthwise. Brush again. Place a heaped spoonful of the cooled spinach mixture close to the corner on the short side. Fold over the other corner to make a triangle, alternating left to right, to encase the filling. Brush all over with more of the melted butter and oil mixture. The result will be a triangular pillow. Bake the triangles for 15–20 minutes until they are crispy and golden all over. Serve hot.

These grilled eggplants always get rave reviews on presentation and taste. For a mezze spread it's nice to have a variety of tasty dishes that look as good as they taste. Try to find the small eggplants for this dish.

Grilled Eggplant with Pomegranate Dressing

6 servings

6 small eggplants (approx. 4 inches long)
olive oil • sea salt • 3 Tbsp butter
1 small onion (or shallot), finely chopped
2 cups pomegranate juice
½ cup chicken stock • 1 Tbsp cornstarch and 2 Tbsp water to make a paste
¼ cup pomegranate molasses
salt and pepper • fresh mint leaves • ½ cup toasted pine nuts
fresh pomegranate seeds

Preheat the oven to 400°F. Peel off several ½-inch strips from the eggplant and slice the eggplant lengthwise in thin slices, keeping the tops intact. Brush all over with olive oil. Fan out each eggplant and press down on it to expose and flatten the insides. Season with sea salt. Roast in the oven for 15 minutes until golden and cooked. Remove to cool.

To make the sauce, heat the butter in a medium saucepan and sauté the onion until soft. Add the pomegranate juice and chicken stock and bring to a boil. Keep on high heat for about 10 minutes to concentrate the flavor and allow some liquid to evaporate. Stir in the cornstarch paste to thicken the sauce slightly. Remove saucepan from heat and stir in the pomegranate molasses. Season with salt and pepper. Place the cooled grilled eggplants on small plates and drizzle some of the sauce on top. Garnish with the mint leaves, toasted pine nuts and fresh pomegranate seeds.

lunch

A bowl of lemony lentil soup with fresh warm bread and a few olives on the side is my favorite lunch. I never like to eat on the run. I believe that whenever you can you should take the time to sit and savor your meals.

Lunch is the main meal of the day in many parts of the globe, including the Arab world. I like to keep it light most of the time. It can be as simple as thin slices of warm shawarma with arugula salad. For me, this is the time of the day I like to have leftovers from the night before.

I find dishes that I can prepare in advance, like baked kibbeh, to be perfect. While it bakes, I prepare a salad like fattouche, et voilà: a wholesome lunch in 30 minutes.

Every culture has its version of the hamburger. In the Middle East many dishes rely on this classic kofta mixture. Lamb, of course, is the meat of choice but beef is also good. Grilling the kofta patties on the barbecue is the best way. Try it in a hamburger bun instead of the pita. The spicy potatoes are delicious with this sandwich. This is my favorite way to cook potatoes. They are full of flavor, and who said potatoes have to be fried to be good? Try this roasting method with other vegetables like eggplants or cauliflower.

Kofta Sandwiches

Makes 6 sandwiches

1 medium onion, finely chopped
1 cup parsley, finely chopped
2 Tbsp tahini • 1 tsp allspice • 1 tsp cinnamon
1 tsp cardamom • ½ tsp ground coriander
2 Tbsp pomegranate molasses
salt and pepper • 1 lb ground lamb
¼ cup peanut oil • 6 small pita breads

tahini and parsley sauce (see recipe on page 86)
sliced tomatoes • sliced red onions
fresh mint leaves, to garnish • parsley leaves, to garnish

Put the chopped onion in a bowl along with the parsley. Add the tahini, spices and pomegranate molasses and mix well. Knead the meat into the flavorful mixture. Form into oval patties and set aside until you're ready to grill them. Meanwhile, make the tahini sauce.

Heat the oil in a frying pan on medium-high heat. Fry the kofta patties about 4 minutes on each side until they're cooked through.

To assemble, open up a pita pocket and place a kofta patty inside. Drizzle on the tahini sauce and add a slice of tomato, onions and some mint and parsley leaves. Serve with the spicy potato wedges.

Spicy Roasted Potato Wedges

6 servings

6 cloves garlic, mashed • ½ cup fresh cilantro, chopped
1 tsp paprika • 1 tsp cayenne pepper
salt and pepper • 2 Tbsp olive oil • 2 Tbsp peanut oil
6 baking potatoes (russets), sliced into wedges

Preheat the oven to 400°F. In a small bowl, mix the mashed garlic, cilantro, paprika, cayenne, salt, pepper and oil. Place the potatoes in a large shallow baking pan and pour the spicy dressing all over. Use your hands to coat them well and spread them out. Roast in the hot oven until they are crisp and golden brown, flipping and shaking them periodically so that they brown evenly. A perfect side dish that goes with anything.

Don't be put off by the number of steps and layers in this recipe. Fattet d'jaj is truly a simple dish. I like to toast the nuts the day before. The yogurt topping can be made ahead and left in the fridge. To save time, I fry large quantities of pita bread and keep them in the freezer. To ensure everything finishes cooking at once, start making the rice ten minutes before the chicken is done. The reward of dipping into the sumptuous layers of crunchy bread, hot rice, lemony chicken and cool yogurt studded with buttery nuts is sublime like nothing else!

Lemony Garlic Chicken with Rice and Yogurt Sauce (Fattet D'jaj)

6 servings

Croutons
2 large pita breads • ¼ cup peanut oil

Yogurt Sauce
3 cups full-fat yogurt • 2 cloves garlic, mashed • sea salt

Chicken Layer
10 cloves garlic, mashed
1 whole chicken (2 lb) • salt and pepper
2 Tbsp peanut oil • juice of 3 lemons

Rice Layer
3 Tbsp clarified butter
2 cups short-grain white rice, presoaked, drained
½ tsp turmeric • sea salt • 4 cups water

¼ cup toasted pine nuts, to garnish
¼ cup toasted chopped pistachios, to garnish
¼ cup toasted slivered almonds, to garnish

Split each pita into 2 rounds and cut into bite-sized squares. In a large frying pan heat the peanut oil and fry the bread squares until crisp and golden. Drain on absorbent paper and set aside.

In a bowl mix the yogurt and mashed garlic and salt to make a sauce and put aside.

Take the 10 cloves of mashed garlic and rub all over the chicken, getting some under the skin. Season with salt and pepper. In a large enough pot, heat the oil and place the whole chicken to brown all over. Pour in all of the lemon juice. Bring the heat down to a simmer, cover and leave the chicken to braise until it falls off the bone (about 40 minutes). Remove all of the skin and bones and discard. Reserve the meat in its lemony sauce.

While the chicken is cooking, it is a good time to make the rice. In a pot, heat the clarified butter and stir in the drained rice. Add the turmeric and salt. Mix well to coat each grain. Pour in the water to cover the rice by 1 inch. Allow to come to a boil. Reduce the heat to a simmer, cover and leave to cook undisturbed until the liquid is absorbed, about 10–15 minutes. Leave covered until ready to serve.

To assemble, place some of the croutons in a serving platter, followed by a layer of the hot rice. Mound the chicken with its lemony sauce on top. Drizzle the yogurt sauce over everything and garnish with the nuts. Serve immediately.

Sweet and sour is a recurring theme in Arabic cuisine. Pomegranate molasses has this distinct taste. Here I've mixed it with other flavors, but it can be used on its own to enhance a salad, a dip or a savory pastry. The pepperiness of the arugula and the soft buttery eggplant along with the sweet cherry tomatoes are unforgettable.

Arugula Salad with Roasted Eggplant and Sweet Pomegranate Dressing

4–6 servings

2 medium eggplants • ¼ cup peanut and olive oil, combined • sea salt

2 tsp whole fennel seeds • 1 clove garlic • ¼ cup balsamic vinegar
¼ cup honey • juice of 1 lemon • 1 Tbsp Dijon mustard
¼ cup pomegranate molasses • ¼ cup extra virgin olive oil

4 large handfuls arugula leaves • 1 small red onion, thinly sliced
2 cups cherry tomatoes, sliced • salt and pepper
½ cup toasted pine nuts • ½ cup fresh pomegranate seeds

Preheat the oven to 400°F.

Peel and cut the eggplants into thick rounds of about 1 inch thick, brush both sides with oil, sprinkle with sea salt and place on a shallow baking sheet. Place in the oven to roast until golden and cooked through, about 15 minutes. Remove, cool completely and slice each round in half. Set aside.

Using a mortar and pestle, crush the fennel seeds and garlic to make a paste. Add the balsamic vinegar, honey, lemon juice, Dijon mustard, pomegranate molasses and olive oil. Whisk together to emulsify the dressing. Set aside.

In a shallow serving platter lay the arugula leaves. Sprinkle the onion, tomatoes, salt and pepper on top. Toss to combine. Scatter the eggplant slices on the salad.

Drizzle some dressing all over. Garnish with pine nuts and pomegranate seeds. Serve immediately, with crusty olive bread and olives on the side.

One of my fondest memories as a child was coming home from school to see a huge mountain of these fritters on the table. There were usually leftovers and they became my lunch for school the next day. My curious friends, who eventually accepted my exotic lunch choices, wanted to know what was in them. I was happy to tell them, "It's cauliflower." Their reactions were of shock that a flower could taste so good. We all munched on my "flower fritters" giggling at the mere idea of eating flowers. Oh, the innocence of childhood!

Cauliflower Fritters with Yogurt and Mint Dip

Makes approx. 16 fritters

1 large head of cauliflower, cut into florets
8 organic eggs • 1 medium onion, grated
4 cloves garlic, mashed • ½ cup parsley, chopped
½ cup fresh cilantro, chopped • 2 tsp cumin
¼ cup rice flour • 2 Tbsp flour • salt and pepper
1½ tsp baking soda • peanut oil for frying

1 cup full-fat yogurt • ½ cup fresh mint, chopped • sea salt

Place the cauliflower florets in a steaming basket and steam until tender. Remove and cool completely. Over a colander use your hands to squeeze out all the water from the cauliflower, letting it fall apart as you do so. I put them in a clean kitchen towel and squeeze hard to get rid of all the moisture. This step will ensure the fritters come out crisp and not soggy.

In a large bowl beat the eggs, onion, garlic, herbs, spices and both flours. Add the salt and pepper. Lastly, tumble in the cauliflower and mix well. Stir in the baking soda.

Heat about a ½-inch layer of oil in a large frying pan. Use a tablespoon to put dollops of the mixture in the hot oil. Cook for 2 minutes on each side until crispy golden and cooked through. Use a slotted spoon to remove the fritters and place on absorbent paper. They are delicious hot or cold.

To make the dip, mix the yogurt and fresh mint in a bowl and season with salt. Serve next to the fritters with a salad on the side.

The easy way of making kibbeh, which is usually fried, is to bake it. The ingredients are exactly the same, except that here I soak the bulgur in hot water, which gives you a kibbeh that is moist and tender. Don't overcook and lose the natural juices of the meat. Serve hot or cold with fattouche salad and yogurt on the side.

Baked Kibbeh

6–8 servings

Filling
¼ cup olive oil
4 medium onions, diced fine
12 oz ground lamb
1 tsp allspice
1 tsp cinnamon
½ cup toasted pine nuts
2 Tbsp sumac
1 Tbsp pomegranate molasses
salt and pepper
½ cup fresh pomegranate seeds

Kibbeh Dough
1½ cups bulgur, fine
about 1 cup hot water
1 medium onion, grated
1 tsp cinnamon
1 tsp allspice
1 tsp dried marjoram
1 tsp cumin
salt and pepper
1 lb lean lamb, from leg
¼ cup olive oil, for brushing pan and kibbeh

In a large frying pan, heat the oil and sauté the onions until soft. Add the meat and toss until brown. Add the spices. Then add the pine nuts, sumac, pomegranate molasses, salt and pepper. Lastly, stir in the fresh pomegranate seeds. Taste to adjust seasonings. Set aside to cool.

Preheat the oven to 350°F. Place bulgur in a bowl and pour the hot water to just cover. In a large mortar and pestle place the grated onion and the spices and make a paste. Add this mixture to the ground lamb and knead by hand. Add the bulgur with its water and mix thoroughly.

Brush a 9- x 13-inch baking dish with oil. Take half of the kibbeh dough and pat down to make a smooth base. Spread the cooled filling on top. Use the rest of the dough to cover the filling by flattening portions in your hands and placing them side by side. The result will be the filling sandwiched between a top and bottom layer of kibbeh dough. Dip your hand in water and smooth out the gaps. Using the back of a knife, make a pattern on the surface of the kibbeh. Brush the top with oil. Bake for 30 minutes.

Fattouche

6–8 servings

5 small pita breads
¼ cup peanut oil
juice of 2 lemons
salt and pepper
2 cloves garlic, mashed
¼ cup extra virgin olive oil
1 small head romaine lettuce
2 handfuls purslane, leaves only (watercress or arugula are good substitutes)
6 radishes, thinly sliced
6 green onions (whites only), thinly sliced

4 Lebanese or Japanese cucumbers, chopped
1 red pepper, chopped
3 cups cherry tomatoes, sliced in half
1 handful fresh mint leaves, chopped
1 handful parsley, chopped
2 Tbsp sumac
pomegranate molasses
½ cup fresh pomegranate seeds

Split each pita so you end up with two disks. Roll up two at a time and cut into ¼-inch strips. Fry in peanut oil until golden and crisp. Drain on absorbent paper.

Make the dressing by combining the lemon juice, salt and pepper, garlic and olive oil. Set aside. Chop all of the vegetables and herbs and place in a large salad bowl, along with the sumac. Scatter in half of the bread strips and leave the rest for garnish. Pour the dressing over the salad and toss with your hands gently to coat evenly. Add more bread strips. Finish with a few drizzles of pomegranate molasses. Lastly, garnish with the fresh pomegranate seeds.

This is an Arab street food like no other. Fragrant and delicious, these sandwiches are an explosion of flavor, enjoying the same popularity as hummus all over the world. My mother used to pack me four falafels for school lunch until my friends caught on how good falafels were. Then, in true Arabian mother form, she would give me a large container full with falafel to feed all of my friends too.

Falafel Sandwiches

Makes approx. 60 falafels

1 cup dried split fava beans (sold with the peel removed), soaked overnight in 3 cups cold water
1 cup dried chickpeas, soaked overnight in 3 cups cold water
1 cup fresh cilantro • ½ cup fresh parsley • 1 medium onion, finely chopped • 1 green onion
6 cloves garlic, minced • 1 small potato, peeled and boiled • 1 Tbsp ground coriander • 1 Tbsp ground cumin
1 tsp cinnamon • 1 tsp allspice • 1 hot red chili, finely chopped • 1 tsp pepper • 1 Tbsp salt
1½ tsp baking soda • ½ cup sesame seeds • peanut oil for deep-frying

pita bread • tahini and parsley sauce • sliced tomatoes • fresh parsley and mint

Drain the fava beans and chickpeas, place in a food processor and pulse until they are coarsely ground. Add the rest of the ingredients (except for the baking soda) and mix until fully combined. Don't overprocess the mixture because you need to keep some texture. Cover and refrigerate for 30 minutes.

Just before frying, add the baking soda. This will make the falafels fluffy on the inside. Heat the oil to 375°F.

I like to use a wok to deep-fry. To ensure the oil is hot, drop a piece of bread in the hot oil and watch it sizzle and float.

Use a falafel tool or use two spoons dipped in oil to shape a single falafel. Dip one side of the falafel in sesame seeds. Next, slowly slide it into the oil. Fry for about 2 minutes until one side becomes golden brown, then flip over to brown the other side. Remove with a slotted spoon and drain on absorbent paper. Serve hot, wrapped in pita bread, with tahini sauce, tomatoes, parsley and mint.

Tahini and Parsley Sauce

2 cloves garlic, mashed • juice of 2 lemons • ½ cup tahini
½ cup yogurt • ½ cup chopped parsley, stalks removed • sea salt

Mix the garlic, lemon juice, tahini, yogurt and parsley until smooth and creamy. Season with salt.

Serve with the falafel or as a dip on its own.

This is a lunch I can put together quickly. The citrus and saltiness of the olive salad are a nice complement to the fish. The fennel seed gives a sweet licorice taste and the sumac adds color and tang. M'hammar is a traditional Emirati sweet rice, made with date molasses, that was often served with fried fish. I've toned down the sweetness by using chopped dates and adding hot pepper.

Roasted Fish with Date and Rice Pilaf, Tomato Salad and Spicy Tomato Salsa

6–8 servings

Date and Rice Pilaf

3 Tbsp clarified butter

1 cup medjool dates, pitted and chopped

1 tsp cinnamon

1 tsp allspice

2 hot red chilies, seeded and chopped

2 cups white basmati rice, presoaked and drained

4 cups chicken stock

zest of 1 orange

6 cardamom pods, lightly bruised

1 cinnamon stick

salt

¼ cup rosewater combined with 2 pinches of saffron

toasted almonds, pine nuts and pistachios, to garnish

cilantro leaves, to garnish

Roasted Fish

1 tsp cumin

1 tsp fennel seeds, crushed in a mortar

1 Tbsp sumac

salt and pepper

6 grouper (hammour) fillets (or any white fish like sea bass or cod), about 1 inch thick with skin

¼ cup vegetable oil

lemon wedges, to serve

Tomato and Olive Salad

2 cups cherry tomatoes, sliced

1 small red onion, thinly sliced

½ cup kalamata olives, sliced

½ handful fresh wild thyme (or fresh oregano)

juice of 1 lemon

3 Tbsp extra virgin olive oil

salt and pepper

Start by making the spicy salsa below. While it cooks, make the pilaf. In a large pot melt the butter and add the dates. Stir in the cinnamon, allspice and chopped chilies. Add the rice and stir to coat each grain. Pour in the chicken stock and allow to come to a boil. Add the orange zest, cardamom and cinnamon, and season with salt. Lower the heat and allow to simmer until rice is done, about 20 minutes. Drizzle in the rosewater and saffron mixture about 5 minutes before the rice is cooked. Do not stir. The rice will be a two-toned white and yellow. Place the cover back on and leave to finish cooking. Garnish with nuts and cilantro before serving.

Preheat the oven to 400°F. Combine all the spices in a small bowl. Brush the fish with oil and coat with the spice mix. Heat a large ovenproof frying pan. Place the fish skin side down and cook for about 4 minutes until the skin is browned and crisp. Turn the fillets over and finish cooking in the oven for approximately 8 minutes. Combine all the ingredients for the salad. Serve the fish with the salsa and salad along with a couple lemon wedges.

Spicy Tomato Salsa (Dakkous)

Makes about 2 cups

2 Tbsp olive oil

6 cloves garlic, mashed

½ cup fresh cilantro, chopped

5 hot red chilies, seeded and chopped

8 ripe tomatoes, peeled and puréed

1 tsp cinnamon

1 Tbsp tomato paste

salt and pepper

2 tomatoes, diced

In a saucepan heat the olive oil and sauté the garlic for 1 minute. Add the cilantro and stir. Add the chilies and tomato purée along with the cinnamon, tomato paste, salt and pepper and allow to come to the boil. Stir in the diced tomatoes. Lower the heat to simmer and leave for 10 minutes to unify the flavors. Serve hot.

*All things small intrigue children. These mini kofta burgers are just the right size for tiny mouths.
I also love to make these especially when I have an all-ladies' lunch since they are easy to eat. It proves that
the best things come in small packages.*

Kofta Burgers with Yogurt, Feta and Mint Sauce

Makes 16 burgers

Kofta
1 lb ground lamb • 1 small onion, finely chopped
½ cup parsley, finely chopped • 1 Tbsp tahini • 1 tsp allspice
1 tsp cinnamon • ½ tsp ground coriander
½ tsp ground cardamom • salt and pepper

Yogurt, Feta and Mint sauce
2 medium cucumbers • 1 cup yogurt • 1 cup labneh (see recipe
on page 181) • 2 cloves garlic, finely minced • ¼ cup fresh mint,
chopped • 1 Tbsp dried mint • 1 cup feta cheese, crumbled

mini pita breads or mini burger buns/rolls
tomatoes, onions and pickles, sliced, to garnish

Combine all the ingredients for the kofta in a bowl. Form into
small patties about the size of a plum and place on a tray. Cover
and refrigerate until you're ready to grill them.

To make the sauce, first seed and grate the cucumbers. Place in
a tea towel and squeeze out all of the water. Place in a bowl and
add the rest of the ingredients for the sauce. Stir to combine.
Taste and add salt if necessary.

Grill the patties on a barbecue (ideally) or griddle pan for
about 3 minutes per side. To serve, place the kofta in a mini
pita or bun and top with the yogurt sauce, tomatoes, onions
and pickles.

Matchstick Potatoes

6 large baking potatoes (russet or Idaho), peeled
peanut oil for deep-frying • sea salt

Using a mandoline preferably, slice the potatoes into
matchstick strips. Place the cut potatoes in a large bowl of
cold water to keep from discoloring. Pour the oil in a deep
pot or wok and heat to 350°F. Drain the potatoes and dry
thoroughly on a clean tea towel. Place a couple of handfuls at
a time in the hot oil and fry until golden and crisp for about
4–5 minutes. Remove and place on a paper towel–lined
shallow pan. Sprinkle with good sea salt while they're hot and
serve immediately.

This is a nice main course salad for lunch. The spices for the meat go well with the peppery arugula, and the sweet and sour vinaigrette pulls it all together. A good way to use leftover shawarma meat.

Warm Shawarma and Arugula Salad with Pomegranate Vinaigrette

4 servings

2 lean sirloin steaks
a pinch each of cumin, coriander, cardamom, cinnamon, allspice, nutmeg, paprika, cloves
salt and pepper • ¼ cup fresh cilantro, finely chopped • 1 tsp zest of lemon
1 tsp zest of orange • 2 Tbsp olive oil • 4 handfuls arugula leaves
1 small red onion, sliced thinly

Vinaigrette
juice of 1 lemon • 1 Tbsp pomegranate molasses
2 Tbsp honey • 1 clove garlic, mashed
salt and pepper • ¼ cup extra virgin olive oil

¼ cup pine nuts, toasted, to garnish
2 Tbsp coarsely chopped pistachios, to garnish

Marinate the steaks in all of the spices, fresh cilantro, zests and olive oil. Rub the marinade all over the meat, cover and leave in the fridge for 1 hour. Take out the meat and allow to come to room temperature. Heat a griddle and grill the steaks, turning over after 5 minutes. Finish cooking the steaks to your liking. Remove and cover lightly with foil to rest for 5 minutes.

While the meat is resting, prepare the vinaigrette by combining all of the ingredients in a bowl and set aside.

To serve, mound the arugula leaves in individual plates. Scatter some sliced onion on each serving. Thinly slice the beef shawarma and place on top. Drizzle on the vinaigrette. Garnish with the pine nuts and pistachios. Serve immediately.

This was the soup my mother made whenever it was raining. She would look outside and say, "Yawm adas," meaning "It's lentil soup day." Comfort food takes us back to a specific time and place. In my case, I would be enjoying a bowl of this lentil soup in my mother's kitchen while watching the rain fall on the windows. A bowl of this creamy yellow soup brightened up the cloudiest days. And, of course, I've carried on the tradition. When the forecast called for clouds and rain my children always knew what they were eating that day.

Creamy Lentil Soup

6–8 servings

2 medium onions, finely chopped • ¼ cup olive oil
2 cups orange lentils, rinsed • 2 large carrots, peeled and grated
¼ cup white rice (arborio, or any short-grain rice)
6 cups chicken stock • 1 tsp cinnamon
½ tsp allspice • 2 tsp cumin • sea salt

Taklia
2 Tbsp olive oil • 4 cloves garlic, minced
¼ cup finely chopped fresh cilantro

¼ cup plain yogurt or sour cream
2 Tbsp fresh cilantro, finely chopped
pita croutons (see recipe on page 13)

In a large pot, sauté the onions in the olive oil until soft. Add the lentils, carrots, rice and chicken stock and bring to a boil. Continue to cook until the soup thickens and lentils fall apart. Stir periodically so that the lentils don't stick. Add the spices and season with salt. Using an immersion blender, purée the soup until creamy.

To prepare the taklia, in a small frying pan heat the olive oil and sauté the garlic for 1 minute until it perfumes the air, then add the cilantro and stir for an additional minute. Pour this on top of the soup, mix in and allow to simmer for 5 minutes to heighten the flavor.

In a small bowl mix the yogurt or sour cream with the cilantro. Place a teaspoon of this on top of each serving of soup. Sprinkle on a few pita croutons. Serve with crusty bread, olives and lemon wedges. A squeeze of fresh lemon juice will brighten the soup.

Grapevine leaves have a natural citrusy taste and go very well with fish. By cooking fish this way some of that citrus note flavors the fish and also the fish is kept moist. Serve this light lunch with the citrus potato salad. You won't miss the mayonnaise.

Sea Bass Wrapped in Vine Leaves

4 servings

juice of 2 lemons • zest of 2 lemons
2 cloves garlic, mashed • 1 tsp cumin
salt and pepper
4 whole small sea bass (or any firm white fish), about 12 oz each

8 large grapevine leaves • olive oil

Mix the lemon juice and zest, garlic, cumin, salt and pepper to make a marinade. Rub all over the fish, cover and set aside for 30 minutes in the fridge. Take two grapevine leaves and place them side by side overlapping (shiny side down).

Place one fish in the center and wrap the leaves around to cover the belly of the fish, leaving the head and the tail exposed. Brush all over with olive oil and grill on a barbecue or bake in the oven at 375°F until done for approximately 15 minutes.

Citrus Potato Salad

4 servings

6 red waxy potatoes • juice of 2 lemons • 1 clove garlic, finely minced
2 green onions, chopped • ¼ cup fresh mint, chopped • 1 tsp sumac
½ tsp chili pepper • ¼ cup parsley (stalks removed), chopped

Wash, scrub and slice the potatoes unpeeled. Steam the potatoes for about 15 minutes (don't overcook).

Make a dressing by mixing all of the remaining ingredients and pour over the warm potatoes. Toss gently and serve alongside the fish.

Fatteh dishes always use a layer of toasted or fried pita bread as part of the recipe. They come in many forms. I like to make my fatteh ensuring that my bread stays crunchy and not soggy. This eggplant version (fatteh beitinjan) is one of my favorites and is an explosion of textures. Don't be put off by the numerous steps. Each part can be made ahead and assembled minutes before serving.

Meat-Filled Mini Eggplants with Creamy Yogurt Sauce

6 servings

Yogurt Sauce
2 cloves garlic • 1 tsp salt • 2 cups thick, full-fat yogurt

12 small eggplants • ½ cup olive oil, divided • 1 medium onion, finely chopped
½ lb lean ground lamb • 1 tsp allspice • 1 tsp cinnamon
2 Tbsp dried mint • salt and pepper • 4 tomatoes, peeled and diced

pita croutons (see recipe on page 13) • ½ cup toasted pine nuts, to garnish • ½ cup toasted chopped almonds, to garnish
a handful fresh pomegranate seeds, to garnish • cayenne pepper or sumac, to garnish (optional)

Start by preparing the yogurt sauce. Crush the garlic and salt in a mortar and pestle and add to the yogurt in a bowl. Mix well and set aside in the fridge.

Trim the stems of the eggplants if they are long, but do not remove the tops. Peel the eggplant in alternating thin strips, resulting in striped little eggplants. Heat the ¼ cup of olive oil in a large frying pan over medium heat and sauté the eggplants until they are golden brown and slightly soft. Keep turning all around. Remove with a slotted spoon and drain on absorbent paper. Leave to cool.

When cool enough to handle, make a slit lengthwise but not through to the bottom, prying open with your fingers gently to make a pocket and set aside.

Meanwhile heat ¼ cup olive oil in a frying pan and fry the onion until translucent and soft. Add the ground meat and brown all over. Season with allspice, cinnamon, mint, salt and pepper. Lastly stir in the diced tomatoes, turn off the heat and leave to cool slightly. Preheat the oven to 350°F. Place a good spoonful of the meat mixture into each eggplant pocket. Lay the filled eggplants in a baking dish and put in the oven to heat through. To serve, put some pita croutons on a serving platter. Arrange the hot stuffed eggplants on top. Drizzle the yogurt sauce on each one and garnish with toasted pine nuts, almonds, fresh pomegranate seeds and a pinch of cayenne pepper. Serve immediately.

Mjadara is the Arabic name for this pilaf. It is a complete meal full of fiber and protein. I love to serve it with a lemony cabbage salad or a simple tomato and onion salad. It is divine for lunch or as one of the choices for a mezze spread. Even cold, mjadara is equally delicious. Take it for your lunch at work instead of a sandwich. I will sometimes substitute bulgur (cracked wheat) for the rice.

Rice and Lentil Pilaf (Mjadara)

4–6 servings

1 cup du Puy (or brown) lentils, rinsed • 4 cups chicken stock
¼ cup olive oil • 1 medium onion, finely chopped
1 cup white basmati rice, presoaked and drained
1 tsp allspice • 1 tsp cinnamon
salt and pepper

½ tsp salt • 2 onions, sliced in thin rounds, to garnish
peanut oil for deep-frying

In a medium pot place the lentils and cover them with the stock. Bring to a boil to cook the lentils until al dente for 10 minutes. Turn off the heat and set aside.

In a large frying pan heat the olive oil and fry the chopped onion until soft. Pour on top of the lentils. Add the drained rice, allspice, cinnamon, salt and pepper. Bring the pot back to the heat and bring everything to a boil. Turn down the heat, cover and leave to simmer for about 12 minutes until all the liquid is absorbed and the rice is fully cooked. Leave covered until ready to serve.

Sprinkle the ½ tsp of salt on the onions and toss. Leave aside for 5 minutes. Wash with cold water and drain well. Place the onions in a clean dish towel and dry completely. Fill a saucepan with about 2 inches of oil and heat until hot but not smoking. Fry the onions until they are crispy and golden. Remove and drain on absorbent paper. Serve the pilaf garnished with the crispy onion rounds.

Lemony Cabbage Salad

4–6 servings

2 handfuls of finely shredded savoy cabbage
(½ a small head)
2 handfuls of finely shredded red cabbage
(½ a small head)
20 cherry tomatoes, sliced in halves
juice of 1 lemon • 2 cloves garlic, mashed
1 Tbsp fresh mint, chopped
1 Tbsp dried mint • salt and pepper
¼ cup extra virgin olive oil

½ cup toasted hazelnuts, coarsely chopped

Place the two kinds of shredded cabbage in a nice serving bowl. Add the tomatoes. Make the dressing by combining the rest of the ingredients. Pour over the salad and toss gently. Garnish with the toasted hazelnuts. Serve immediately.

When I was growing up, my mother would always have an assembly line of these mini "meat'zas" coming out of the oven. We would devour them before the next batch was even out of the oven. The herbs in the filling along with the pomegranate molasses give these meat flatbreads a distinctive taste. I have also included a recipe for a second filling made with my favorite ingredient, eggplant. Warning: you can't eat just one! A bowl of creamy yogurt and an Arabian Garden Salad (see recipe on page 131) complete this meal.

Meat or Eggplant Flatbreads

Makes 24 flatbreads

Dough
6 cups flour

2 Tbsp instant dry yeast

1 tsp salt

1 Tbsp sugar

½ cup plain yogurt

¼ cup olive oil

2½ cups lukewarm water

Meat Filling
1 lb lean ground lamb (from leg)

2 onions, finely chopped

2 tomatoes, seeded and diced small

½ cup fresh parsley, finely chopped

½ cup fresh mint, finely chopped

3 cloves garlic, mashed

1 tsp allspice

1 tsp cinnamon

3 Tbsp tahini

2 Tbsp pomegranate molasses

salt and pepper

3 hot chilies, seeded and finely chopped (optional)

Eggplant Filling
½ cup olive oil

1 onion, finely chopped

2 cloves garlic, minced

1 tomato, chopped

2 medium eggplants, cut into 1-inch cubes

2 Tbsp fresh mint, chopped

2 hot chilies, seeded and chopped

salt and pepper

4 oz feta cheese cut into small cubes

To make the dough, in a large bowl mix all the dry ingredients and stir to combine. Add the yogurt, olive oil and water in the center of the flour. Gradually work the flour mixture to make a dough. Knead the dough on a work surface for about 5 minutes, until soft and elastic. Place in a lightly greased bowl, cover with a damp cloth and leave to rise for 1½ hours until doubled in size.

For the meat filling, in a large bowl mix all the ingredients together. Use your hands to combine well. Preheat the oven to 400°F. Roll out one-quarter of the dough to about a ¼-inch thickness, cut into about six 4-inch rounds and place on a greased baking sheet. Repeat with another one-quarter of the dough. Place a generous amount of the meat filling on each dough circle and press gently to spread evenly. Pinch the edges to make a border. Bake in the oven until the meat is cooked and the dough is lightly golden, about 15–20 minutes.

For the eggplant filling, in a large frying pan heat ¼ cup of olive oil and sauté the onions and garlic until soft and translucent. Add the tomato and stir in gently. Remove from the heat and set aside to cool. In another frying pan, heat ¼ cup of olive oil and sauté the eggplants until cooked and lightly browned. Sprinkle on the chopped mint, chili, salt and pepper. Remove from the heat and allow to cool completely. Add the onion and tomato mixture. Stir in the feta cheese and taste to adjust seasonings. Roll out the rest of the dough into 12 rounds and spread a heaping spoonful on each round. Pick up the right and left sides, bring together in the center and pinch to seal, leaving the two ends exposed. Bake in a preheated oven until done and lightly golden, about 15–20 minutes.

This is one of my favorite soups. It's hearty and full of healthy ingredients. I've used du Puy lentils because they keep their shape but you can use any brown lentil. When red Swiss chard is available I like to use it since it adds a vibrant color to the soup. Swiss chard is lemony and goes well with the earthiness of the lentils and potatoes, but spinach is a good substitute. The lemon juice lifts and brightens the taste of the soup, and the classic Arabic tradition of adding taklia to many stews and soups makes it even more fragrant and flavorful.

Lemony Lentil Soup with Swiss Chard

6-8 servings

¼ cup olive oil • 2 medium onions, finely chopped
1½ cups du Puy lentils • 5 cups chicken stock
4 medium potatoes, peeled and diced
3 handfuls sliced Swiss chard • 1 tsp allspice
salt and pepper • taklia (see recipe on page 94)
juice of 1 lemon or more

In a large pot heat the olive oil. Add the onions and sauté until slightly soft. Stir in the lentils. Pour in the stock, bringing up to a boil. Skim off the foam that floats to the surface. After 5 minutes add the diced potatoes and Swiss chard. Season with allspice and salt and pepper. Turn down the heat and simmer until the potatoes and lentils are cooked.

Prepare the fragrant taklia, add it to the soup and leave to simmer for 5 minutes. Taste to see if it needs more salt and adjust the seasoning. Turn off the heat. Just before serving, pour in the lemon juice. Serve with nice crusty bread on the side and more lemon wedges.

This tart is my version of mou'sakhan, a traditional Palestinian dish. The onions have to be cooked slowly in the best oil to caramelize. I like to serve my tart with a fresh thyme and arugula salad, and yogurt on the side. Lunch couldn't be better.

Caramelized Onion Tart with Sumac Roast Chicken

6 servings

Pastry

2½ cups flour • 2 tsp cracked black pepper
pinch of salt • 1 tsp sugar
1 cup unsalted cold butter, cut into small cubes
3 Tbsp cold water • 1 egg

Topping

½ cup olive oil • 8 medium onions, sliced thinly
4 cloves garlic, sliced • salt and pepper • 1 Tbsp sugar
small handful of fresh thyme (leave some to garnish)
2 Tbsp sumac plus extra to coat the chicken
3 chicken breasts, on the bone • olive oil • salt and pepper
fresh pomegranate seeds • ½ cup toasted pine nuts

In a bowl put the flour, black pepper, salt and sugar and mix. Put in the cold butter cubes and using your fingers rub the butter into the flour to make a crumbly consistency. Make a well in the center and pour in the water and egg. Bring the flour gradually together and mix quickly to make a smooth dough. Flatten slightly into a disk and cover with plastic wrap. Refrigerate for 1 hour until ready to use.

Preheat the oven to 375°F. Roll out the pastry to fit two 13- x 4-inch tart pans with a removable bottom. Prick the base with a fork. Chill in the fridge for 20 minutes. Line the pastry with parchment paper (or foil), fill with dried beans to prevent it from rising and blind bake for 15 minutes. Remove the beans and paper, turn down the oven temperature to 350°F and bake for an additional 15 minutes until they have a light golden color. Cool the pastry completely. Remove from the pan, place on flat serving platters and set aside.

Put the olive oil in a large heavy-based pot. On medium heat sauté the onions and garlic. Sprinkle in the salt, pepper and sugar. Stir to coat the onions well and turn down the heat to low. Add the fresh thyme. Cook gently, stirring, taking care not to burn them. The onions will caramelize and sweeten as they cook. This will take about 40 minutes. When they are meltingly soft, remove from the heat and stir in the sumac. They will turn a pinkish color. Pour into a colander sitting in a bowl to drain the excess oil.

Preheat the oven to 375°F. Coat the chicken with olive oil, salt, pepper and sumac. Roast for about 30–40 minutes. When done, remove, cover lightly with foil and leave to rest.

To assemble the tart, spread the caramelized onions on the pastry. Remove the chicken from the bones, thinly slice and place on top of the onions. Garnish with pine nuts and a few fresh thyme sprigs and pomegranate seeds.

Arugula and Thyme Salad

1 handful fresh wild thyme (or fresh oregano),
washed and drained
2 cups arugula leaves • ½ red onion, sliced thin
2 green onions, chopped
20 cherry tomatoes, sliced in half

1 clove garlic, mashed • juice of 2 lemons
extra virgin olive oil • 1 Tbsp sumac • salt and pepper

Place the fresh thyme and arugula leaves in a nice salad bowl. Add the onions. Scatter the tomatoes on top. Make the dressing by mixing the mashed garlic, lemon juice and olive oil. Pour over the salad. Sprinkle on the sumac, salt and pepper. Toss gently to coat evenly. Serve as a side salad or add a few cubes of feta cheese on top and enjoy it as a complete meal in itself.

dinner

This is the meal when more than likely the family is gathered together at the end of the day. Parties are usually focused on dinner. This is the time to wow your friends and family with something amazing.

Good home cooking is what Arabic food is all about. It is comfort food par excellence. But more than anything, the Arabian table is about generosity and choice.

My mother used to make what seemed like an endless number of dishes when we had guests because she didn't want anyone to be disappointed. "The eyes have to be full before the stomach" was her motto. I am definitely my mother's daughter, but I've learned not to overdo it. I like to choose one elaborate dish like the eggplant pilaf and serve simpler complementary dishes with it.

Your guests will always appreciate the effort you went through to make them a meal. That is the greatest compliment.

My daughter Mimi loves this Cornish game hen recipe but only when I make toum alongside it. I've included the recipe for this highly addictive garlic dip. She scoops the dip and places the smallest sliver of chicken before she takes a bite. I think she likes the chicken too! Here I serve this with a bulgur and freekeh pilaf. Tabbouleh (see recipe on page 46) would also be a wonderful salad to have with the chicken.

Barbecued Cornish Hens

6–8 servings

4 Cornish game hens, approx. 1 lb each
½ cup yogurt • ½ cup crushed toasted walnuts
¼ cup olive oil • juice and zest of 1 lemon
4 cloves garlic, mashed • 1 tsp ground cardamom
1 Tbsp thyme • ½ cup fresh cilantro, chopped
2 tsp chili powder (optional)

Mimi's Toum
10 cloves garlic • 1 tsp sea salt
juice of 1 lemon • ½ cup olive oil
2 Tbsp water

juice of 1 lemon

Prepare the chicken by cutting out the backbone and pressing on the chest to flatten. Mix all of the ingredients to make a marinade. Rub all over the chickens, cover, and refrigerate for at least 4 hours.

To make the toum, place all the ingredients except the oil and the water into a small food processor and purée. While the motor is running, pour in the olive oil in a slow steady stream. The sauce will come together and look like creamy mayonnaise. Lastly, add the water. Store in the fridge.

Fire up the barbecue and grill the chickens on a medium heat until golden and tender on the inside, around 30 minutes. Squeeze some lemon on top of the cooked chicken 2 minutes before removing from the grill. Serve immediately with bulgur and freekeh pilaf, a salad and the toum in which to dip the chicken.

Bulgur and Freekeh Pilaf

6–8 servings

¼ cup olive oil • ½ red onion, chopped
1 cup bulgur, coarse, rinsed in cold water and drained
1 cup freekeh, rinsed in cold water and drained
3 cups chicken stock • 1 tsp allspice
salt and pepper • zest of 1 orange
½ cup dried pomegranate seeds (or dried cranberries),
soaked in juice of 1 orange • ½ cup dried apricots, sliced
½ cup pine nuts, toasted • ½ cup chopped pistachios, toasted
½ cup slivered almonds, toasted

fresh pomegranate seeds • fresh parsley

In a medium pot, heat the olive oil and sauté the onion until soft. Add the bulgur and freekeh and stir to coat each grain. Pour in the chicken stock, allspice, salt, pepper and orange zest. Add the soaking pomegranate seeds and juice, and the apricots. Bring to a boil. Lower the heat to a simmer and add half the pine nuts, pistachios and almonds, saving the rest for garnish. Cover and leave to cook for about 15 minutes.

When done, mound on a platter and garnish with the rest of the nuts, fresh pomegranate seeds and parsley leaves. Serve hot or room temperature as a side dish with chicken or any meat. This pilaf paired with a salad makes a great and healthy lunch.

My mother used to tell me how much she missed mloukhiya (jute mallow) when she first moved to Canada. Now it is widely available frozen, dried and fresh in Middle Eastern supermarkets. It's a tender leaf that doesn't require a lot of cooking. A part of the jute family, it has an earthy taste that works well with chicken or meat. The taklia is essential to the finish of this comforting stew. Mloukhiya is delicious with a final squeeze of lemon to brighten it up. Serve with vermicelli rice.

Jute Mallow and Chicken Stew

6–8 servings

2 Tbsp vegetable oil • 1 whole chicken (3 lb) • 8 cups water
2 onions, sliced into quarters • 2 cinnamon sticks
2 bay leaves • 6 cardamom pods, bruised
2 lb mloukhiya leaves (fresh or frozen), washed and drained
1 tsp ground coriander • 1 tsp ground cinnamon
1 tsp ground allspice • salt and pepper

¼ cup clarified butter • 20 cloves garlic, sliced thin
1 cup fresh cilantro, chopped coarsely

In a large pot heat the vegetable oil and sauté the whole chicken to brown all over. Pour in the water and bring to a boil. Skim off the scum that floats to the surface and discard. Add the onions, cinnamon sticks, bay leaves and cardamom pods. Continue to cook gently, covered, for 45 minutes until the chicken is cooked. Strain the stock using a colander set over a second pot. Remove the chicken and debone. Set the meat aside. Return the stock to the heat, stir in the mloukhiya leaves (if you're using frozen leaves, you can add them without defrosting) and allow to come to a boil. Add the ground spices, salt and pepper. Lower the heat and cook on medium heat for 15–20 minutes.

In a frying pan heat the butter, sauté the garlic for 1 minute and add the cilantro. Allow to cook together for an additional 3 minutes. Pour over the mloukhiya stew and let simmer for 10 minutes more. Remove from the heat and drop in the reserved chicken. Serve hot with a squeeze of lemon, chopped cilantro and vermicelli rice on the side.

Vermicelli Rice

6–8 servings

¼ cup clarified butter
1 cup vermicelli pasta (I use Italian semolina pasta)
2 cups white basmati rice, presoaked, rinsed and drained
4 cups water • sea salt

Break apart the vermicelli into small pieces. In a heavy-bottomed pot heat the butter and sauté the vermicelli until golden brown. Stir in the drained rice, and stir for 1 minute to coat each grain. Pour in the water and salt and allow to come to the boil. Reduce the heat to a simmer, cover and leave to cook for approximately 15 minutes until all of the water is absorbed and the rice is cooked. Turn off the heat and keep covered until ready to serve.

Meat and vegetables are served in many inventive ways in the Middle East. By far one of the most delightful is cooking a range of foods in yogurt. We, like our Turkish neighbors, love yogurt. Some people claim it to be the secret to living a long life. The zucchini in this dish can be prepared a day ahead and cooked in the yogurt the next day. Follow the instructions carefully to stabilize the yogurt.

Stuffed Baby Zucchini in Herb Yogurt Sauce

4–6 servings

2 Tbsp olive oil • 1 onion, diced fine
10 oz ground lamb, from leg
1 tsp cinnamon • 1 tsp allspice
salt and pepper • ½ cup pine nuts, toasted
12 zucchini (about 4 inches), washed and cored
¼ cup vegetable oil

Yogurt Sauce
8 cups full-fat yogurt • 5 Tbsp cornstarch • ¼ cup cold water

Taklia
2 Tbsp clarified butter • 10 cloves garlic, minced
¼ cup fresh cilantro (or mint), chopped

½ cup toasted pine nuts, to garnish

To make the filling, heat the olive oil in a large frying pan and sauté the onion until soft and translucent. Add the ground lamb to brown, stirring continuously. Season with cinnamon, allspice, salt and pepper, and lastly add the pine nuts. Turn off the heat and allow to cool. Drain the zucchini and fill with the meat and nut mixture. In a large frying pan heat the vegetable oil and sauté the filled zucchini until lightly brown on all sides. Place on absorbent paper and prepare the yogurt sauce.

Put the yogurt into a large 6-quart pot over medium heat. Whisk the yogurt to make it creamy. Stir the cornstarch in ¼ cup of cold water to make a paste and add to the yogurt. With a wooden spoon, stir continuously until the yogurt has stabilized and thickened. Gently put in the zucchini to finish cooking in the yogurt, about 20 minutes.

The last step is to heat the clarified butter in a small frying pan and sauté the garlic for 1 minute; add the cilantro and sauté for another minute. Set aside some for garnish. Pour this on top of the yogurt and zucchini and allow to simmer for 5 minutes. Remove the zucchini and place in a serving dish. Pour some yogurt sauce on top, garnish with more of the taklia and toasted pine nuts. Serve with rice on the side.

How to core zucchini: *Take off the stem of each zucchini. Cupping one zucchini with one hand, hold and puncture the cut top with a zucchini corer (a "kousa corer") about halfway down. Pull out and repeat next to the first cut, going all the way around. Move the corer in a circular motion to release the pulp. Hold on firmly to the zucchini and continue to insert the corer more deeply and gently scrape away more of the pulp, always working in a circular motion. Try to take out as much of the pulp as possible without puncturing the skin. Place the finished zucchini in a bowl of cold water to keep from turning brown until all are done.*

There is an endless choice of stews in Arabic cuisine. This is one of my favorites. Try to find baby okra, which has fewer seeds and looks much prettier. My mother used to squeeze a little lemon over the stew at the end of cooking. I like to add the citrus notes of lemon and orange by just adding the zest. Like any stew it's good served with rice or potatoes and even couscous.

Baby Okra Stew

6–8 servings

¼ cup vegetable oil • 2 lb leg of lamb, cut into cubes
2 onions, sliced thin • 6 cups water
2 cinnamon sticks • 2 bay leaves • 4 cardamom pods, bruised

¼ cup vegetable oil • 2 pkgs baby okra (14 oz each), frozen
1 can (28 oz) tomatoes, puréed • 2 Tbsp tomato paste
zest of 1 orange • zest of 1 lemon • 2 Tbsp sugar

Taklia
2 Tbsp clarified butter • 10 cloves garlic, sliced thin
1 handful fresh cilantro, chopped
8 tomatoes, peeled and diced

In a large, 6-quart pot heat ¼ cup vegetable oil and brown the lamb all over. Add the onions and stir for 2 minutes. Pour in the water, bring to a boil and skim off the scum from the surface. Add the cinnamon sticks, bay leaves and cardamom. Lower to medium heat and cover to cook until the meat is tender, for about 40 minutes. Strain in a colander over another pot, keeping the stock. Remove the meat and leave aside.

Quickly rinse the frozen okra in cold water to get rid of any ice crystals. In a large frying pan, heat ¼ cup vegetable oil and sauté the okra until crisp all over. Drain on absorbent paper. Set aside. Place the pot of reserved stock on medium heat and add the tomato purée, tomato paste, orange and lemon zest, sugar and the reserved meat. Put the okra into the tomato sauce.

In a small frying pan heat the clarified butter and sauté the garlic for 1 minute. Add the cilantro and cook for an additional minute. Pour this taklia on top of the stew. Stir gently to combine. Lower the heat and leave to simmer for 10 minutes more. Lastly, stir in the fresh diced tomatoes and simmer for 5 minutes and remove. Serve hot with vermicelli rice (see recipe on page 112).

Layered Fragrant Rice Pilaf

1 cup sultana or golden raisins, soaked in ½ cup rosewater
1 tsp cinnamon • 1 tsp cardamom
½ cup toasted slivered almonds
½ cup toasted chopped pistachios
½ cup dried pomegranate seeds (or dried cranberries)
zest of 1 orange • ½ cup dried apricots, chopped

5 cups water • 2 tsp salt
2 cups white basmati rice, presoaked, drained

¼ cup oil • 2 pinches of saffron soaked in 2 Tbsp rosewater and
2 Tbsp orange flower water • ½ cup hot water
2 Tbsp clarified butter
toasted pine nuts, pistachios and almonds, to garnish
a handful fresh pomegranate seeds, to garnish

Drain the sultanas, mix with cinnamon and cardamom and set aside. In another bowl, combine the nuts with the pomegranate seeds, orange zest and apricots and set aside.

In a medium pot boil the water and salt. Pour in the rice to blanch for 5 minutes. Remove and pour into a colander to drain.

In a 2-quart pot heat the oil and start by putting in a layer of the semicooked rice. Sprinkle the sultana mixture on top. Add more rice, then a layer of the nuts and dried fruits, then more rice. Continue alternating layers, finishing off with the rice. Drizzle on the saffron and its flower waters in a swirly pattern on top of the rice. Don't stir. Lastly, pour in ½ cup hot water. Place a tea towel on the pot and place the cover on top. Gather the towel up over the lid and away from the flame (a technique often used in the Middle East to trap the steam and allow each grain of rice to remain fluffy and separate). On the lowest heat leave the rice to cook and steam undisturbed for about 30 minutes. Garnish with toasted nuts and pomegranate seeds. Serve alongside any stew or roast chicken, lamb or fish.

Shawarma is Middle Eastern street food that is undeniably delicious. Traditionally, tender lamb is marinated in a special blend of spices and roasted on a vertical grill. As it cooks, thin slices of succulent meat fall only to be picked up and laid to rest on a bed of lettuce and tomatoes inside a waiting warm pita. A drizzle of special tahini sauce is the final touch before rolling it up and taking that first delicious bite. I make my home version of this unforgettable sandwich using either lamb or chicken (and sometimes beef). You won't want to go out for shawarma anymore!

Shawarma (Lamb or Chicken)

12 or more servings

Lamb Shawarma
1 tsp each of cinnamon, paprika, cardamom, cumin, cayenne pepper, ground coriander, allspice, ground cloves, nutmeg
½ tsp mastic ground with 1 tsp of salt
juice and zest of 1 orange • juice and zest of 1 lemon
1 cup fresh cilantro, chopped • ¼ cup olive oil
salt and pepper
1 fresh leg of lamb (about 4 lb), boned and butterflied, trimmed of excess fat

plenty of pita bread
tahini and parsley sauce (see recipe on page 86)
1 cup fresh mint and parsley
2 tomatoes, sliced, or a handful of red or yellow cherry tomatoes, sliced in half • 12 pickled gherkins, if desired

Chicken Shawarma
6 cloves garlic, mashed
juice of 2 lemons • zest of 1 lemon • ¼ cup olive oil
3 bay leaves, broken
1 tsp each of paprika, ground cinnamon, nutmeg and allspice
2 cinnamon sticks, broken • 2 tsp cardamom
½ tsp cumin • ½ tsp cloves
½ tsp mastic ground with ½ tsp salt
6 skinless, boneless chicken breasts

toum (see recipe on page 111) • plenty of pita bread
1 cup fresh mint and parsley • 2 tomatoes, sliced
pickled gherkins, if desired

For the lamb shawarma: Mix all of the dry and wet ingredients with the olive oil to make a marinade in a large glass bowl. Place the butterflied leg of lamb in the marinade and rub it all over. Cover with plastic wrap and leave in the fridge overnight to soak up all the flavors.

Take out the meat and allow to come to room temperature. Fire up the barbecue. Place the prepared meat on the grill over medium heat for a total of 45 minutes if you like it medium rare, turning it halfway. Leave it to cook longer if you like it more well done. I prefer the meat tender and pink in the middle. When ready, remove the shawarma and cover loosely with foil and allow to rest for 15 minutes before slicing.

To assemble the lamb shawarma sandwich, slice the rested meat into thin slices. Fill a pita with the meat, drizzle over some tahini sauce, place a few leaves of fresh mint and parsley and some tomato slices or a few halves of cherry tomatoes, and roll it up. Even a couple of baby gherkins are yummy with it.

For the chicken shawarma: Combine all of the ingredients in a large glass bowl to make a marinade. Place the chicken breasts in the bowl and rub the marinade all over. Cover and leave in the fridge overnight. When ready to grill, heat the barbecue and place the chicken to cook on medium heat until done. Remove and cover with foil to allow the meat to rest for 5 minutes. Slice into thin strips.

To assemble the chicken shawarma sandwich, spread some toum on a small pita. Place a few slices of chicken and herbs like mint and parsley and roll it up. A slice of tomato and pickles on the side completes this meal.

This meal is great served with various dips, vegetables, spicy potato wedges and plain yogurt flavored with a little chopped fresh mint.

Maqlouba in Arabic literally means "upside down." I remember one Sunday our family was going on a picnic to the park. But we weren't going to have hot dogs and hamburgers. A salad was packed and two pots sat waiting, one full with homemade yogurt and the other with maqlouba (still right side up). I was worried we would be the joke of the day when people saw how we ceremoniously flip our pot of rice and eggplant and then eat copious amounts of yogurt with it. Our favorite spot was taken by a large family of Italians who had even larger pots bubbling over with pasta and tomato sauce. What a beautiful sight! A family cooking their traditional food and celebrating their culture, not embarrassed the least bit. My mother flipped her perfectly cooked maqlouba and we shared our food with our Italian neighbors. I learned a valuable life lesson that day: I share and celebrate the food of my heritage every chance I get and think nothing of taking pots to a picnic anymore.

Maqlouba (Meat and Rice with Eggplant)

8–12 servings

4 large eggplants • ½ cup vegetable oil
4 lb lamb (from leg), cut into large cubes
4 onions, sliced thin • 2 celery stalks, coarsely sliced
1 leek, sliced (whites only) • 2 cinnamon sticks
2 bay leaves • 6 cardamom pods, bruised slightly
4 allspice berries (whole) • 6 cups cold water

¼ cup vegetable oil • 2 Tbsp butter
2 cups baby carrots (or 4 large carrots, sliced)
1 tsp cinnamon • 5 Tbsp vegetable oil
3 cups white basmati rice, presoaked and drained
2 tsp ground cinnamon • 2 tsp ground allspice
½ tsp turmeric • some hot water, if needed

½ cup pine nuts, ½ cup almonds and ½ cup pistachios,
toasted, to garnish • ½ cup fresh pomegranate seeds
a few sprigs of mint, to garnish

All of the components can be made ahead and the maqlouba assembled an hour before serving. Preheat the oven to 400°F. Peel the eggplants and slice lengthwise, approximately ½ inch thick. Brush both sides with ¼ cup of the vegetable oil and lay on a baking sheet in one layer. Roast on the lowest rack until golden brown on both sides. Remove and set aside to cool.

In a large pot heat ¼ cup of oil and brown the meat all over. Take a handful of the sliced onions and sauté for 1 minute. Add the celery, leek, cinnamon stick, bay leaves, cardamom, and allspice berries. Pour the cold water to cover the meat and allow to come to a boil, skimming off the scum on the surface. Lower the heat to medium and cover to cook the meat until tender, for about 40 minutes. Strain the stock into another pot using a colander. Reserve the meat aside. Discard all of the vegetables.

While the meat is cooking, in a large frying pan heat ¼ cup vegetable oil and fry the remaining onions until golden and sweet. Remove and drain on paper towels. In another pan, heat the butter and sauté the carrots until lightly golden, for about 2 minutes. Remove, sprinkle with 1 tsp cinnamon and set aside.

In a large 8-quart pot, place the eggplants along the bottom and sides of the pot next to each other overlapping slightly, going all the way around. Gently place the cooked lamb in the bottom as the first layer. Add the carrots, then scatter the fried onions over. Mix the cinnamon, allspice and turmeric into the drained rice and spoon over the carrot layer. Lastly, ladle the reserved stock to cover the rice completely. You might need to top it up with more water to cover the rice by 2 inches. Bring to a boil. Reduce the heat to a simmer, cover and leave until the rice is cooked and the liquid is absorbed. It will take about 20 minutes. Remove from the heat and leave the maqlouba covered for at least 30 minutes to rest before serving. Take a large platter bigger than the pot and turn the pot upside down on it. Very slowly lift off the pot taking care not to topple the layers. Garnish with all of the toasted nuts, pomegranate seeds and mint. Serve immediately with cool yogurt and the Arabian Garden Salad on page 131.

I can still remember coming home from school on many cold, snowy days in Ottawa and being greeted by the comforting aroma of these cabbage rolls. Cabbage is always available in the winter months, which is why my mother made it so often, although it might have also been because it was my father's favorite dish.

Braised Stuffed Cabbage in Lemon Garlic Sauce

6 servings

30 cabbage leaves (preferably savoy) • 2 cups short-grain white rice, presoaked, drained
¼ cup clarified butter • 1 tsp cinnamon • 1 tsp allspice • 2 Tbsp dried mint • salt and pepper
10 oz ground lamb • 2 Tbsp butter • 20 cloves garlic, sliced thinly • salt
4 cups chicken stock • ½ cup lemon juice

To prepare the cabbage leaves for stuffing, separate each leaf from the core. Fill a large pot halfway with water and bring to a boil. Take 5 leaves and plunge into the water to blanch for 2 minutes to soften. Remove and drain in a colander. Continue until all are done. When cool, take one leaf and carefully slice off the protruding middle rib to achieve a flat-looking leaf. Be careful not to cut through the cabbage leaves. Set aside to make the filling.

In a bowl combine the rice, butter, cinnamon, allspice, 1 Tbsp of the dried mint, salt and pepper, mixing well. Add the ground lamb and combine well. Lay one leaf on your working surface shiny side down and place about 2 Tbsp of filling on it. Start to roll away from you, folding over the sides to the middle to completely encase the filling. It's like making spring rolls. You will have a cigar shape in the end. (You may also wish to leave the sides open.) Continue using all the cabbage leaves and set aside.

In a 5-quart pot heat 2 Tbsp of butter and sauté half the sliced garlic for 2 minutes. Remove from the heat and start placing the filled cabbage leaves seam side down on top of the garlic. Keep them close together and layer one on top of the other. Sprinkle some salt, 1 Tbsp dried mint and a scatter of uncooked sliced garlic. Keep layering in the same way. Pour in the chicken stock to cover the cabbage rolls. Place a heatproof plate on top to keep everything in place. Return to the heat and bring to a boil. Cover, lower the heat and leave to cook gently for about 40 minutes. About 10 minutes before they are done, remove the plate and pour in the lemon juice and a sprinkle of dried mint.

Carefully lift the cabbage rolls out and drizzle on the lemony sauce left in the pot. Serve hot with a cool bowl of yogurt and mint with a wedge of lemon.

Pasta dishes aren't common in the Arabic kitchen but I'm glad shish barak is. I've added
Swiss chard to the sauce for added color. I've also been known to take a shortcut by using wonton wrappers.
But when I'm in the mood I will make the dough from scratch.

Meat-Filled Pasta in Herb Yogurt Sauce (Shish Barak)

6–8 servings

Meat Filling
¼ cup olive oil
1 onion, chopped finely
10 oz lean ground lamb
1 tsp allspice
1 tsp cinnamon
1 Tbsp dried mint
salt and pepper
½ cup pomegranate seeds
½ cup toasted pine nuts

wonton wrappers, at least 40,
or homemade dough

Dough
2 cups flour
pinch of salt
1 tsp baking powder
¼ cup vegetable oil
1¾ cups lukewarm water

Yogurt Sauce
¼ cup vegetable oil
1 onion, chopped finely
4 cloves garlic, minced
4 handfuls sliced Swiss chard
salt and pepper
1 cup chicken stock
5 cups full-fat yogurt
5 Tbsp cornstarch, mixed
with ½ cup water

Taklia
2 Tbsp clarified butter
10 cloves garlic, sliced thinly
½ cup fresh cilantro

pine nuts, to garnish

Preheat the oven to 350°F.

Filling the homemade dough: Place approximately ½ teaspoon of the meat filling in the middle of each round of dough. Fold over into a crescent, bring the two ends together and pinch to seal. It will look like a tortellini. Place on a baking sheet and put in the oven to dry and harden slightly, for approximately 5 minutes. Remove and set aside until ready to cook in the yogurt sauce. Extras can be frozen at this stage for future use.

Wonton wrappers: Separate each one and place flat on your surface. Place the filling to one side. Brush water on one corner and fold over to seal completely. Repeat to fill as many as you can (it depends on the size of the wonton wrapper: I use 4-inch-square ones). Place in the preheated oven to dry them slightly, for approximately 5 minutes. Cool completely.

In a frying pan, heat the oil and sauté the onion and garlic until soft. Add the Swiss chard, salt, pepper and stock. Leave to cook for about 10 minutes. Remove and set aside.

In a large pot on medium heat, pour in the yogurt and whisk to make it creamy. With a wooden spoon, stir continuously. Mix in the cornstarch paste and continue stirring until the yogurt thickens. Add the cooked chard with its liquid along with the filled dough. Bring to a boil, then lower heat to simmer for about 5 minutes until the pasta is cooked through.

Just before serving, in a small frying pan heat the clarified butter and sauté the garlic slightly without browning for 1 minute. Add the fresh cilantro and sauté for 1 more minute. Pour this taklia over the yogurt. Carefully place the pasta on a serving platter. Spoon the yogurt sauce on top and garnish with pine nuts. Serve hot.

To make the meat filling, heat the oil in a frying pan and sauté the onions until soft. Add the meat and brown all over. Season with the allspice, cinnamon, dried mint, salt and pepper. Remove from the heat and stir in the pomegranate seeds and pine nuts. Set aside while you prepare the dough or the wonton wrappers.

To make the dough, in a bowl mix the flour, salt and baking powder. Add the liquids and mix in to form a dough. Knead a couple of minutes until soft and pliable. Cover and set aside to rest for 30 minutes. Using half the dough, roll out as thin as possible and use a cookie cutter to make 3-inch rounds.

Samaki har'ra is a dish that is very popular in the Arab world, especially in Lebanon and particularly in the port city of Tripoli. While my version may not look traditional, the taste is truly authentic. It's definitely something a little different from the usual salmon dish. Sea bass or snapper are also good fish for this recipe.

Walnut and Herb–Stuffed Salmon with Spicy Tahini Sauce

4–6 servings

**two 1 lb salmon fillets, skin on, center-cut and trimmed to be the same size
1 tsp cinnamon • ½ cup walnuts, toasted
4 cloves garlic, minced
½ cup fresh cilantro, chopped coarsely
½ cup flat-leaf parsley, chopped coarsely
juice of ½ lemon • zest of 1 lemon
4 hot red chilies, seeded and chopped
1 tsp paprika • 1 tsp cumin • ¼ cup extra virgin olive oil
salt and pepper • kitchen twine**

Preheat the oven to 375°F. Prepare the salmon fillets by trimming the extra thin belly part. Use tweezers to pull out any bones. Blot dry and sprinkle half of the cinnamon on the meat side of each fillet and set aside to make the filling.

In a food processor, place the walnuts, garlic, cilantro, parsley, lemon juice and zest, chilies, paprika, cumin, cinnamon, olive oil, salt and pepper. Pulse a couple of times until all the ingredients are chopped. Don't overprocess – try to keep a slightly coarse texture.

Place one fillet skin side down on a working surface and place enough of the spicy walnut filling to fully coat the fish. Cover with the other fillet skin side up. Using the kitchen twine, gently tie up the fish to ensure the filling stays in place. Drizzle olive oil in the baking dish and put in the prepared fillet, drizzling a little more oil on top. Season with salt and pepper. Bake for about 20–25 minutes until done. Serve with the rice tabbouleh and the spicy tahini sauce on the side to drizzle over the cooked fish.

Spicy Tahini Sauce

**1 cup tahini • ½ cup water • juice of 2 lemons • 2 Tbsp olive oil
4 cloves garlic, minced • ½ cup fresh cilantro, chopped
4 hot red chilies, seeded and chopped
sea salt • ½ cup toasted pine nuts**

In a small bowl mix the tahini, water and lemon juice until creamy (it should look like smooth cake batter) and set aside. In a saucepan, heat the olive oil and sauté the garlic for 1 minute, then add the cilantro and hot chilies and stir for another minute. Pour in the tahini mixture and whisk to combine. Season with salt to taste. It should be a creamy pourable consistency – add a small amount of water if needed. Allow to simmer for 5 minutes to let the flavors mingle. Remove from heat and stir in the toasted pine nuts. Serve hot.

Rice Tabbouleh

4–6 servings

**1 cup white basmati rice • 2½ cups hot water • 1 Tbsp salt
1 Tbsp of olive oil • tabbouleh (see recipe on page 46)**

Soak the rice for 1 hour in cool water. Drain it and place in a saucepan. Pour in the hot water and salt. Allow to boil for 5 minutes. Take off the heat and pour the hot rice into a colander to drain. Spread the rice on a clean lint-free tea towel to completely cool and dry. Preheat the oven to 375°F. Turn the dry rice onto a baking sheet. Drizzle on the oil and using your hands toss to coat and spread out evenly. Bake in the hot oven for 15 minutes to crisp the rice slightly. This will give it a nutty taste. Make the same tabbouleh recipe on page 46, substituting the crispy rice for the bulgur. This is also a good way to use leftover rice. Brown rice and wild rice are delicious alternatives.

Lamb is the meat of choice in the Middle East. These racks are coated with fresh herbs and pistachios. They're crunchy on the outside and succulent and tender on the inside. I've paired this elegant cut of meat with an arugula and tomato salad. The peppery and citrusy arugula leaves go well with the sweetness of the lamb. The moussaqa'a on page 66 is also a perfect match.

Herb and Pistachio–Crusted Rack of Lamb

4 servings

2 racks of lamb (cleaned, French trimmed and patted dry)
2 Tbsp olive oil • salt and pepper
½ cup butter, room temperature
1 cup fresh parsley • ½ cup fresh cilantro
1 tsp ground allspice • 1 tsp paprika
6 cloves garlic, mashed • zest of 1 lemon
1 cup fresh breadcrumbs (white bread, crusts removed)
1 cup pistachios, ground but not too fine

Preheat the oven to 400°F. Rub the lamb all over with olive oil and season with salt and pepper. Put the racks on a baking pan with the meat side up and roast for 15 minutes. Remove to cool but leave the oven on and lower the temperature to 350°F.

In a food processor, place the butter, parsley, cilantro, allspice, paprika, garlic and lemon zest and pulse a couple of times. Then add the breadcrumbs and pistachios and continue to pulse to incorporate, ensuring that it remains coarse. Spoon the herb and nut mixture on top of the lamb, meat side up, and, using your hands, pat down to stick.

Return the lamb racks to the oven and finish roasting for another 15 minutes. Remove and cover loosely with foil and leave to rest for 5 minutes before serving.

Arugula and Tomato Salad

4 servings

juice of 1 lemon • 2 Tbsp sumac
extra virgin olive oil

4 handfuls of arugula leaves, washed and drained
20 cherry tomatoes, sliced in half
2 Lebanese or Japanese cucumbers, seeds removed, sliced
1 small red onion, sliced thinly • salt and pepper
pomegranate molasses

Make the dressing by combining the lemon juice, sumac and olive oil.

Place the arugula leaves in a salad bowl, and add the tomatoes, cucumbers and onion. Pour on the dressing, season with salt and pepper and toss to combine. Lastly drizzle on some pomegranate molasses. Serve immediately.

I have made this roast chicken recipe for many dinner parties and it's always a hit. The stuffing is full of nuts and dried fruits and it really looks good on the table. I especially cherish a memory of when my dear friend Coco's son, Ramzi, was visiting. He was six at the time. I made this chicken and he ate and ate and savored every morsel. Then he said, "This is the best chicken I ever tasted, can you give my mum the recipe?" Well here it is, and in my heart it will always be Ramzi's Roast Chicken.

Roast Chicken with Rice, Fruit and Nut Stuffing

4–6 servings

Brine Bath for the Chicken
3 cinnamon sticks • 2 bay leaves • strips of zest of 1 orange
½ cup salt • ½ cup sugar • ½ cup honey
enough water to immerse the whole chicken
one 5–6 lb chicken

3 Tbsp vegetable oil • 1 onion, diced • 10 oz ground lamb
1 tsp cinnamon • 1 tsp allspice • salt and pepper
1 cup short-grain white rice, presoaked, drained
3 cups chicken stock • ½ cup chopped pistachios, toasted
½ cup pine nuts, toasted • ½ cup slivered almonds, toasted
½ cup dried apricots, coarsely chopped
½ cup dried pomegranate seeds

2 Tbsp vegetable oil • 1 tsp cinnamon • 1 tsp paprika
salt and pepper • kitchen twine to tie the legs
¾ cup stock or water
fresh pomegranate seeds, to garnish

Start the brining process the night before. Mix all of the ingredients for the brine in a large enough bowl to accommodate the chicken and make room in the fridge to keep overnight. When you are ready to stuff the chicken, take it out of the brine and pat it dry.

To make the filling, heat the oil in a large frying pan and sauté the onion until soft. Add the lamb and stir until it browns. Sprinkle in the spices, salt and pepper. Stir in the rice. Pour in the chicken stock and allow it to come to a boil.

Reduce the heat to a simmer, add some of the nuts and fruits, leaving some for garnish. Cover and leave to cook for 10 minutes. The rice will finish cooking in the oven. Uncover and put aside to cool completely.

Preheat the oven to 400°F. Spoon as much of the stuffing that will fit loosely in the cavity of the chicken. Reserve the rest of the filling to finish cooking later. Rub the whole chicken with 2 Tbsp oil, cinnamon, paprika, salt and pepper. Tuck back the wings behind the neck and tie the legs together with the kitchen twine. Place in a big enough roasting pan. Bake in a preheated oven until done, for approximately 1 hour.

To finish cooking the remaining stuffing, add in a little more stock or water, cover and leave to simmer about 10 minutes more until the rice is done. Garnish with fresh pomegranate seeds and serve alongside the roast chicken.

Arabian Garden Salad

5 handfuls of romaine lettuce, sliced
4 small cucumbers, seeds removed and sliced
4 small green onions, sliced
2 cups cherry tomatoes, sliced in half
1 red pepper, chopped • 6 radishes, thinly sliced
1 handful of fresh mint, finely sliced
1 handful parsley, stalks removed, chopped
2 cloves garlic, mashed • juice of 2 lemons
½ cup extra virgin olive oil • salt and pepper • 1 Tbsp sumac

Cut all the vegetables and herbs and place in a large salad bowl. Make the dressing by combining the mashed garlic, lemon juice and olive oil. Pour the dressing, salt, pepper and sumac and mix by hand to coat evenly. Enjoy immediately.

Kofta is ground meat, usually lamb, mixed with onion and fresh herbs like parsley and mint, and seasoned delicately with a few spices. There are many versions. This one is a delicious way to use tahini. Tahini has a nutty and earthy flavor and the orange zest and juice cut through that. My mother used to whip this up at the last minute and have it on the table in half an hour before the guests arrived, as she was never satisfied with the endless number of dishes she had already prepared! My Arabian Garden Salad on page 131 and the Vermicelli Rice on page 112 would complete this meal.

Ground Lamb in Tahini Citrus Sauce

6-8 servings

4 medium potatoes, sliced into ½-inch rounds • ½ cup peanut oil • 2 lb ground lamb
1 onion, finely chopped • ½ cup parsley, finely chopped • 1 tsp cinnamon
1 tsp allspice • salt and pepper

1 cup tahini • juice of 2 lemons (or more) • juice of 1 orange
zest of 1 orange • 2 cups water • sea salt

½ cup pine nuts, toasted • a handful of chopped parsley, to garnish

Peel, wash and slice the potatoes into rounds. Heat the peanut oil in a large frying pan and fry the potatoes until golden on both sides. Remove and place on absorbent paper to cool.

Preheat the oven to 350°F.

In a large bowl, combine the ground lamb, onion, parsley, cinnamon, allspice, salt and pepper. In a baking dish, place the potatoes in one layer.

Shape the kofta into long sausages (about 6 inches) and place on top. Bake in the oven for 10 minutes until partially cooked. Remove. Keep the oven on while you make the sauce. Mix the tahini, lemon juice, orange juice, orange zest, water and salt to taste. It should be a pourable consistency and creamy. Pour the sauce all over and return to the oven to finish cooking and to thicken the sauce slightly, about 20 minutes. Garnish with toasted pine nuts and parsley. Serve hot with white rice and a salad.

There is something comforting about knowing you have meat marinating in the fridge from the night before. Half the work is already done. Skewer the chunks of seasoned meat and place on the barbecue grill. Have ready all of your condiments, side dishes (couple of dips from the mezze chapter) and plenty of fresh pita bread to slide the meat into and devour.

Shish Kebab and Shish Tawouk

6-8 servings

Shish Tawouk (Chicken)
2 lb boneless chicken breasts, cubed
10 cloves garlic, mashed
salt and pepper
1 tsp cinnamon
1 tsp allspice
1 tsp smoked paprika
1 tsp ground cardamom
juice of 1 lemon
zest of 1 lemon
¼ cup olive oil
½ cup plain yogurt
1 Tbsp tomato paste
½ cup fresh cilantro, finely chopped
½ cup walnuts, finely chopped

Shish Kebab (Lamb)
1 tsp cinnamon
1 tsp allspice
1 tsp ground coriander
juice of 1 lemon
¼ cup olive oil
2 lb cubed lean lamb, from leg
1 cup dried apricots
12 small onions or shallots

Marinate the chicken with all of the marinade ingredients for at least 4 hours in the fridge. Put chicken pieces on a skewer. Grill on a barbecue until cooked and tender. Serve with toum (see page 111).

Marinate the lamb in the spices, lemon juice and oil for at least 4 hours in the fridge. Put lamb pieces onto a skewer with one onion and a couple of apricots in between the meat cubes. Grill on barbecue until cooked.

Freekeh Pilaf

4-6 servings

1 cup freekeh • ¼ cup olive oil
½ red onion, finely chopped
1 can (14 oz) tomatoes, puréed

5 tomatoes, chopped
1 tsp allspice
1 tsp cinnamon
salt and pepper

Put the freekeh in a bowl, cover with water and wash well. Change the water and drain the freekeh a couple of times to get rid of any sediment. Drain and leave aside.

In a 2-quart pot, heat the oil and sauté the onion until soft and translucent. Add the freekeh and stir to coat the grains. Add in the puréed and chopped tomatoes. Season with allspice, cinnamon, salt and pepper. Allow to come to a boil. Lower the heat and cover. Leave to simmer for about 15 minutes until the freekeh is done. It will be soft but still al dente. Serve hot or at room temperature beside any grilled meat or fish.

Beet Salad

4-6 servings

6 medium beets
2 Tbsp vegetable oil
2 handfuls fresh wild thyme (or fresh oregano)
juice of 1 lemon

juice and zest of ½ orange
1 clove garlic, mashed
1 Tbsp sugar • sea salt
¼ cup fresh mint, chopped

Preheat the oven to 400°F. Rub each beet with a little oil and wrap each one individually with foil. Place on a baking pan and roast for approximately 1½ hours. Remove and unwrap. Leave until cool enough to handle. Put on some gloves and peel the beets. Slice into paper-thin slices. Arrange on a platter or individual small dishes. Scatter on the fresh thyme leaves.

To make the vinaigrette, whisk together the lemon juice, orange juice and zest, garlic, sugar and salt in a bowl. Drizzle onto the salad and garnish with the fresh mint.

Stuffing vegetables is an art relished by most people in the Middle East. Peppers are easy to fill while others, like cucumbers, carrots and turnips, can be a bit more challenging. Humble vegetables are elevated to another level once stuffed and served with the appropriate sauce. I love making stuffed peppers since their shape acts as the perfect vessel for any filling. Try a colorful yellow and red pepper combination.

Stuffed Peppers

6 servings

3 red peppers • 3 yellow peppers
2 cups short-grain white rice, rinsed and drained
2 Tbsp clarified butter • 2 tsp cinnamon • 2 tsp allspice
4 cloves garlic, minced • 3 Tbsp dried mint • salt and pepper
10 oz ground lamb • 6 slices of tomatoes • 2 Tbsp olive oil
6 cloves garlic, sliced thinly • 8 large tomatoes, peeled and puréed
1 cup water • ¼ cup tomato paste • ½ cup fresh mint, chopped
¼ cup parsley, chopped • fresh mint, chopped, to garnish

Cut the tops of the peppers carefully with a knife, leaving the stem intact. Remove the membrane and seeds. Keep the tops as they will be the lids. Rinse and leave aside to prepare the stuffing.

In a large bowl place the rice, butter, 1 tsp of the cinnamon, 1 tsp of the allspice, minced garlic, 2 Tbsp of the dried mint, salt and pepper, mixing well. Add the ground lamb and, using your hands, mix it into the rice. Fill the hollow peppers loosely two-thirds full leaving the rice plenty of room to expand and place 1 tomato slice on top. Cover with the top of the pepper. Repeat for all peppers. Place the filled peppers in a deep baking dish.

Preheat the oven to 375°F.

In a saucepan heat the olive oil and sauté the sliced garlic for 1 minute and pour in the puréed tomatoes. Add the water, tomato paste, 1 Tbsp dried mint, fresh mint, parsley, 1 tsp cinnamon, 1 tsp allspice, salt and pepper. Taste to adjust seasonings. Pour the tomato sauce all around the peppers. Cover with foil and bake in the preheated oven for 45 minutes until rice is cooked. Serve hot with the tomato sauce and a sprinkle of fresh chopped mint.

This is one of those dishes people never forget. They will gasp with delight at your architectural skills. Believe me, this is a one-pot wonder! You can prepare the whole dish the night before and place it on the stove to cook the next day. Cooking it at a slow simmer ensures the best results.

Stuffed Vine Leaves, Zucchini and Lamb Chops Braised in Lemon Juice

8–12 servings

2 cups short-grain white rice, presoaked, drained
2 Tbsp melted clarified butter • 2 tsp allspice
1 tsp ground cinnamon • 1 Tbsp dried mint
salt and pepper • 1 lb ground lamb, from leg
12 small zucchini, scrubbed and cored (see instructions on page 115)
1 jar (1 lb) grapevine leaves, rinsed, drained, stems removed, leaves cut in half

2 lb lamb chops (rib chops or loin chops), trimmed of excess fat • salt and pepper
1 tsp cinnamon • 1 tsp allspice • 2 Tbsp dried mint
2 Tbsp vegetable oil • 10 tomatoes, chopped
2 cups fresh lemon juice • 1 cup water

In a bowl place the drained rice, clarified butter, allspice, cinnamon, dried mint, salt and pepper into a bowl. Add the ground lamb and use your hands to mix it in well. Fill each zucchini loosely three-quarters full, and set aside. Proceed to fill the vine leaves with the same mixture. See instructions on page 65.

Season the lamb chops with salt and pepper, cinnamon, allspice and 1 Tbsp of dried mint. Heat the vegetable oil in a 6-quart pot. Brown the lamb cutlets on both sides a few at a time. Remove and continue with the rest. When all are done, lay them back in the same pot side by side to cover the bottom. Take a handful of the chopped tomatoes and scatter over the meat. Place the zucchini on top of the potatoes, tightly side by side radiating out from the center. Scatter more tomatoes and a pinch of salt. Place the stuffed vine leaves on top, seam side down, with their short ends touching the edge of the pot,

forming a circle. Work toward the center. Keeping them close together will help keep their shape. Keep lining them up and make a second layer with the rest of the stuffed leaves. Sprinkle some salt and dried mint. Scatter in the last of the tomatoes and pour in all of the lemon juice and water. Place a heatproof plate (or pot lid smaller than the pot) on top of the vine leaves. Press down gently to secure everything. This will help keep the vine leaves in place. Bring to a boil for 5 minutes. Turn the heat down to a low simmer. Cover and leave to cook slowly for approximately 2 hours. Remove from heat and leave covered for 30 minutes to rest before serving.

Take a large platter with a rim and place upside down over the pot. Flip over and leave for 10 minutes before slowly lifting up to reveal the multilayered dish. Garnish with lemon slices. Serve hot with salad and mint yogurt.

Sayyadieh is one of those dishes I love to make whenever I'm having a big dinner party. I like to serve it family style, showcasing all of the succulent fish. Use any fish that is meaty. Frying the onions is the secret to getting rice that has color and exceptional flavor. This salad is delicious with any fried or grilled fish.

Fish and Rice Pilaf with Fried Onions (Sayyadieh)

8–12 servings

2 lb sea bream fillet (6 pieces)

2 lb salmon fillet (6 pieces)

2 tsp cumin

2 tsp ground coriander

1 tsp paprika

salt and pepper

a handful of flour

½ cup peanut oil

½ cup peanut oil

8 medium onions, thinly sliced

8 cups fish stock or chicken stock

1 tsp ground coriander

1 tsp cumin

1 tsp turmeric

1 tsp cinnamon

salt and pepper

3 Tbsp clarified butter

4 cups white basmati rice, presoaked, drained

a good pinch of saffron threads

1½ cups toasted pine nuts

fresh pomegranate seeds

Season the fish with the cumin, coriander, paprika, salt and pepper. Dredge with flour. In a large frying pan heat ½ cup peanut oil and fry the fish until golden crisp on both sides and cooked through. Remove and place on paper towels to drain. Set aside while you prepare the onions and rice.

In a large frying pan over medium heat pour in ½ cup of peanut oil and fry the onions in batches until crispy and golden brown. Be careful not to burn. Remove the onions and drain on absorbent paper. Set aside a big handful for the garnish.

Heat the stock in a large pot and drop in the fried onions to release their brown color and sweetness. Remove onions with a slotted spoon, place them in a food processor and pulse a couple of times to break them into a chunky paste. Season the stock with the coriander and cumin, turmeric, cinnamon and salt and pepper. Taste to adjust the seasoning.

In a large 6-quart pot heat the butter and add the drained rice. Sprinkle in the saffron threads. Add the puréed onions and 1 cup of the toasted pine nuts and stir well to combine. Pour enough of the seasoned stock to cover the rice completely. Allow to come to a boil. Reduce heat, cover and let simmer until the rice is cooked and all of the liquid is absorbed (about 25–30 minutes). You may need to add some more stock or water. Turn off the heat when it is done and keep covered to rest before serving.

Preheat the oven to 375°F. Reheat the cooked fish in the oven before serving on top of the rice. Garnish with the remaining pine nuts and reserved crispy onions. Two handfuls of fresh pomegranate seeds are the perfect finish. Serve with *dakkous* (Spicy Tomato Salsa – see the recipe on page 89).

Mixed Citrus Salad

6–8 servings

1 pink grapefruit

3 oranges

3 limes

6 lemons

1 red onion, thinly sliced

¼ cup fresh parsley, thinly sliced

¼ cup fresh mint, thinly sliced

salt and pepper

juice of 1 orange

3 Tbsp extra virgin olive oil

Peel all the citrus fruit by first cutting off the tops and bottoms. Place the fruit on the cutting board and slice off the peel in strips, removing the white pith. Go all the way around. Cupping the fruit in one hand and using a very sharp paring knife, cut out the segments lengthwise to release them between the membranes. Place all the fruit on a nice serving platter. Add the onion slices. Scatter the parsley and mint. Season with salt and pepper. Mix the orange juice and olive oil and drizzle on top of the citrus fruit. Serve immediately.

desserts

I can spend the entire day making desserts. My mother picked up on that when I was young, so she made me the official pastry chef in the family. I started baking in an Easy-Bake oven and I quickly earned the right to use the real oven. My attempts were not always a success, but with my mother's encouragement there was always a next time and I delighted in the challenge. I haven't looked back since.

Arabs adore sweets but in reality only serve them on special occasions. Fresh fruit usually ends a big meal. Pastries and cookies can be served with tea or coffee anytime of the day. Chocolate-filled cardamom cookies (see page 149) are ideal.

I love Arabic sweets. Rose flower-scented syrup is commonly drizzled over a variety of buttery pastries, like baklawa or nammoura. The fillings can be nuts, dates or luxurious fresh cream. One of my favorites is knafe nabulsieh, a crisp shredded pastry filled with cheese, glistening with sweet syrup. A delectable ending to any dinner.

This homemade version of Arabian pistachio ice cream will make you want to eat it every night. Sahleb (also spelled "salep"), a powder made from tubers of wild orchids, is the thickening agent in this ice cream as there are no eggs in the recipe. It also gives it a smooth and chewy texture. Real sahleb is not sold outside of Turkey, but there are sahleb mixes with a similar flavor available – you may be able to find it in Turkish grocery stores or online. The crème fraîche gives this ice cream a nice tang. I've also included the technique for making ice cream without a machine.

"A Thousand and One Nights" Pistachio Ice Cream

Makes 2 quarts

one 7 oz pkg sahleb (I like Cortas brand)
½ tsp mastic ground with ¼ cup sugar
½ cup cold milk • 4 cups full-fat milk
1 cup heavy cream • 1 cup sugar
2 Tbsp rosewater • 1 Tbsp orange blossom water
1½ cups crème fraîche or heavy cream
½ cup chopped pistachios, soaked in ½ cup rosewater
½ cup chopped pistachios

Dissolve the sahleb and mastic-sugar mixture in ½ cup cold milk to make a paste and set aside. Pour the milk and cream in a large saucepan and place on medium heat. Stir in the 1 cup sugar to dissolve and allow to come to a boil. Whisk in the sahleb and mastic paste. Using a wooden spoon continue to stir until the milk thickens and coats the back of the spoon. Remove from the heat and mix in the rosewater and orange blossom water. Place a sieve over a large glass bowl and pour the hot thickened mixture through to strain. Whisk in the crème fraîche, and drain the pistachios and mix in. Allow to cool completely in the fridge. Put into an ice cream machine and follow the manufacturer's instructions. Fold in the chopped pistachios just before placing in the freezer.

Making ice cream without a machine

Make sure the ice cream mixture has completely cooled in the refrigerator. Place the mixture in a stainless steel bowl and put in the freezer. When it becomes partially frozen (that is, the sides and bottom are almost firm and the middle is still liquid), take out the ice cream and, using a wire whisk, beat the mixture vigorously to incorporate air and break up the ice crystals, until it becomes creamy. Return the bowl to the freezer and repeat the process 4 or 5 times more, beating vigorously each time. Lastly, transfer the ice cream to a freezerproof container, and cover and freeze until ready to serve.

Nammoura is a lovely semolina cake. There are no eggs in it so it doesn't rise much. Rose-scented syrup is poured over the cake while it is still hot and left to absorb. It remains moist, sweet and delicious for days. This was my mother's go-to dessert whenever we had guests. We always wished we had visitors more often.

Sweet Semolina Cake (Nammoura)

Makes 30 pieces

3 cups semolina, medium • 1 cup semolina, fine
½ tsp mastic ground with 2 Tbsp sugar
1 cup sugar • ½ tsp salt
1 cup clarified butter, melted
¼ cup rosewater • 1 cup yogurt
1½ tsp baking soda • ¼ cup tahini • blanched almonds
3–4 cups of rose syrup (see recipe on page 181)

In a large bowl mix the semolina, ground mastic, sugar and salt together. Stir to combine well. Add the melted butter and rub into the semolina with your fingers. Whisk in the rosewater, yogurt, and baking soda to make a thick batter.

Coat the bottom and sides of a 12 x 16-inch baking pan with the tahini. Ladle in the batter. Wet your hands and spread it out on the pan evenly. Smooth the batter and leave aside for 30 minutes. Preheat the oven to 375°F. Score the surface in a diamond or square pattern, and place an almond in the center of each diamond or square. Bake in the preheated oven for 1 hour until golden brown and firm to the touch. Remove, and while hot, immediately pour the cool syrup all over the cake. It will seem a bit excessive when you see the puddle forming in the bottom. Leave the nammoura at least an hour to soak up the syrup properly. It is best eaten completely cooled.

Cardamom is a spice that is used widely in the Arab world, both in savory and sweet dishes, and it is the secret flavor in the fragrant Arabic coffee. In these cookies, cardamom gives an exotic taste that goes very well with chocolate. Use any cookie-cutter shape you like!

Chocolate-Filled Cardamom Cookies

Makes 2 dozen filled cookies

1½ cups unsalted butter, room temperature • ½ cup icing sugar
1 tsp vanilla • 2 cups flour
½ tsp baking powder • ¼ cup cornstarch
1 tsp ground cardamom • pinch of salt

Chocolate Filling
1 cup heavy cream
2 cups chopped semisweet chocolate
5 Tbsp unsalted butter

icing sugar to dust

In a large bowl beat the butter and icing sugar until creamy. Add the vanilla. Sift the flour, baking powder, cornstarch, cardamom and salt, and add to the butter mixture. Mix together to form a dough. Shape the dough into two disks, wrap in plastic wrap and refrigerate for 1 hour.

Preheat the oven to 350°F. Take out the dough and roll on a lightly floured surface. For the photo I used star and moon cookie cutters to cut an equal number of cookies. Just make sure to make two of each shape to sandwich the chocolate filling.

Place on parchment-lined baking sheets and bake for 15 minutes until lightly golden. Leave to cool completely.

To prepare the chocolate filling, in a small saucepan heat the cream just until boiling. Remove from the heat and pour in the chocolate pieces. Stir to melt. Whisk in the butter.

Spread the chocolate filling on half of the cookies and place the other same-shaped cookie on top. Dust lightly with icing sugar just before serving.

After a full day of fasting during the holy month of Ramadan, these atayef are a welcome treat. Like all traditional foods associated with special holidays, somehow they taste best at the right time. But that shouldn't stop you from making these unforgettable moreish sweets at anytime of year. And by moreish *I also mean Moorish, with a flavor and fragrance that is exotic, complex, and evocative of a culture that goes back to ancient times. These are divine.*

Cheese- or Walnut-Filled Crepes (Atayef)

Makes 24 crepes

Walnut Filling
1 cup walnuts, chopped coarsely • 5 Tbsp sugar
zest of 1 orange • 2 tsp cinnamon
2 Tbsp orange blossom water

Cheese Filling
10 oz akkawi cheese (desalted) or ricotta mixed with half
of the mozzarella • 3–4 oz fresh mozzarella cheese, grated
5 Tbsp sugar • 1 Tbsp rosewater

2½ cups flour • pinch of salt
1 Tbsp sugar • 1 tsp instant dry yeast
3 cups lukewarm water • 1 tsp baking soda
2 cups of rose syrup (see recipe on page 181)
peanut oil, for deep-frying • ½ cup ground pistachios, to garnish

To prepare the walnut filling, mix the walnuts, sugar, zest, cinnamon and orange blossom water. Set aside. To prepare the cheese filling, I start the process the night before. Desalt the akkawi cheese by slicing thin and immersing in cold water, leaving it to soak. Drain and change the water again after 1 hour, repeating five or six more times to get rid of all the salt. Taste the cheese before using it to ensure no saltiness remains. Mix the 2 cheeses, sugar and rosewater and set aside in a colander to drain any excess water.

Put the flour into a large bowl. Mix in the salt, sugar and yeast. Pour in the water gradually and beat vigorously with a whisk.

Beat in the baking soda. The batter should be creamy and pourable. Cover and leave aside to rise for 1 hour. Spread a clean lint-free tea towel on a cookie sheet and set aside. Heat a nonstick heavy-bottomed frying pan. Whisk the batter a little before ladling ¼ cup in the pan to make 4-inch disks. Cook only on one side. Bubbles will start to form; they are ready when there are no more shiny wet spots on the top (about 1–2 minutes). Place each atayef, browned side down, on the tea towel to cool completely.

Take one atayef and cup it in your hand. Fill it with either one of the fillings. Bring the edges together to form a crescent, pinching around the edges with a little firmness to keep the filling enclosed. Fill the remaining and set aside while you prepare your "workstation." Pour 2 cups of rose syrup in a deep bowl. Line a plate with paper towels. Heat the oil in a heavy-bottomed saucepan to 350°F on the thermometer. Deep-fry the filled atayef no more than four at a time until golden brown on both sides. Remove with a slotted spoon and place on the paper towels. While hot, slide a couple at a time into the cool syrup for 1 minute to absorb. Remove with another slotted spoon. Serve hot, garnished with pistachios.

Baking option
Preheat oven to 400°F. Place the atayef in a shallow baking dish. Brush with clarified butter (see page 181) on both sides. Bake until golden and crisp, turning over halfway. Remove and pour the cool syrup over the hot atayef. Garnish with pistachios.

I remember my mother would lovingly make this for us during the coldest Canadian winters. We were curious to know who Umm Ali (which means "Ali's mother") was. We tried to imagine what she might have looked like and had many laughs at the possibilities. We decided in the end that she must have been an amazing mother to think of making a dessert so luxurious and comforting for her children. This pudding has an exceptional texture because I use filo and puff pastry. And the flavor . . . so moreish.

Umm Ali
(Arabian Bread Pudding)

10–12 servings

10 oz filo pastry • ¼ cup clarified butter, melted • 10 oz puff pastry
¾ cup sultana or golden raisins (soaked in ½ cup rosewater)
¾ cup chopped pistachios • ½ cup dried apricots, sliced thinly
¾ cup almonds, sliced and toasted
4 cups full-fat milk • 2 cups heavy cream • 1 cup sugar
1 vanilla pod, split and with seeds scraped • 2 Tbsp rosewater
1 Tbsp orange blossom water
½ cup heavy cream, lightly whipped
½ cup icing sugar
toasted almonds and pistachios, to garnish

Preheat the oven to 325°F. Take 4 or 5 sheets of filo pastry and lightly brush each sheet with the melted butter. Lay them on a large baking sheet. They do not need to be flat so you can crumple them up slightly to fit. Bake until golden and crisp. Remove to cool. Continue with the rest of the filo, 4 or 5 sheets at a time. Place the rolled-out puff pastry on another baking sheet and bake, following the package instructions, until puffed and crisp. Remove to cool.

In a deep 8-inch-round baking dish place several layers of filo and a large piece (or pieces) of puff pastry for the first layer, keeping the filo and puff pastry intact as much as possible. Sprinkle with some sultanas, nuts and apricots. Add more layers in the same order until done. In a large saucepan heat the milk, cream, sugar and the scraped vanilla pod and seeds.

Allow to come to a boil for 2 minutes. Take it off the heat and add the rose and orange blossom waters. Remove the vanilla pod, and carefully and gradually pour the hot cream/milk over the pastries. Leave it for 10 minutes to soak up all the liquid. Top with the whipped cream and sprinkle icing sugar and bake for 40 minutes until the top browns and becomes puffed up. Remove and leave to sit for 10 minutes. Garnish with toasted almonds and pistachios at the last minute. Serve hot straight from the pan. I sometimes make individual portions in ramekins. The time in the oven will be reduced by half.

Many versions of baklawa are enjoyed all over the Middle East. Different countries like to claim it as their own, and who can blame them? This is a dessert like no other. The Arab world shares a colorful history with all its neighbors and many dishes have crossed borders. Baklawa is simply scrumptious, especially with a cup of strong coffee. Making it at home lets you control the sweetness. Use only the freshest nuts and only clarified butter. Baklawa should remain the color of ivory. This is my version of this world-famous pastry.

Baklawa

Makes 4 dozen pieces

5 cups pistachios, coarsely ground
¾ cup sugar • 2 Tbsp orange blossom water • 2 Tbsp rosewater
2 pkgs filo pastry (1 lb each), defrosted in the fridge the night before (Apollo is my favorite brand)
2½ cups clarified butter, melted
4 cups rose syrup (see recipe on page 181) • ¾ cup pistachios, finely ground

Prepare the filling by combining the ground pistachios, sugar, orange blossom and rose waters and set aside.

Take out the filo pastry and leave it to come to room temperature while still sealed in the package. Preheat the oven to 350°F. Set up your workstation by laying out the filo pastry and covering it with a slightly damp cloth. Put the melted butter into a deep bowl and use a pastry brush to coat a 12- x 18-inch rimmed baking sheet (about ½ inch deep). Take one sheet of the filo pastry and lay it in the pan. Dip one hand in the butter and sprinkle over the filo sheet. Using the same hand tap the pile of dough to pick up the top sheet and place it in the pan and sprinkle with butter again. Continue until half of the sheets are used (the equivalent of 1 pkg). Spread the pistachio filling to cover the filo pastry right to the edges of the pan.

Continue layering and sprinkling butter in between each sheet of filo pastry using the rest of the filo. Finish by coating the top generously with melted butter. Using a very sharp knife, cut through to the bottom of the baklawa into long lengthwise strips and then on an angle to make diamond-shaped slices.

Bake in the preheated oven for about 1½ hours. Oven temperatures vary. Keep a watchful eye on the baklawa: as it bakes, the layers will begin to puff up, becoming crisp. Don't allow the baklawa to brown; it should be an ivory color. Sometimes I place a sheet of foil lightly on top to prevent it from browning. Remove the finished baklawa and while hot immediately pour on the cool syrup. Garnish each piece with a pinch of the finely ground pistachios. Leave to cool and fully absorb the sweet syrup. Serve at room temperature.

All the flavors and textures in the famous baklawa are in this cheesecake.
You will love every exotic mouthful of this classic dessert with an Arabian touch.

Baked Baklawa Cheesecake

10-12 servings

Crust
½ cup walnuts, coarsely ground • ½ cup sugar • 2 tsp cinnamon
8 sheets filo pastry • ½ cup melted butter

Cake
5 pkgs (½ lb each) cream cheese, room temperature
1½ cups sugar • ¼ cup honey • ¼ cup cornstarch
pinch of salt • zest of 1 orange • 1 Tbsp orange blossom water
1 Tbsp rosewater • 5 eggs • 3 egg yolks • ½ cup heavy cream
¾ cup walnuts, coarsely chopped • 1 tsp cinnamon • ¼ cup sugar

6 sheets of filo pastry, to decorate
¼ cup rose syrup (see recipe on page 181) • ¼ cup pistachios, coarsely chopped

Combine the walnuts, sugar and cinnamon in a small bowl. Set aside. Brush one sheet of filo pastry with melted butter and lay it on the bottom of an 8-inch springform pan, going up the sides and letting it hang over the edges. Sprinkle some of the nut mixture on the pastry. Keep layering the pastry, with the excess hanging over the edge, and the nut mixture until all of the pastry dough is used.

Preheat the oven to 400°F.

In a large bowl beat the cream cheese, sugar, honey, cornstarch, salt, orange zest, orange blossom water, rosewater and 2 of the eggs until creamy. Add the rest of the eggs and the yolks one at a time. Beat in the heavy cream, on the lowest speed if using an electric mixer. Pour half of the batter into the prepared pan. Sprinkle the walnuts, cinnamon and sugar on top and ladle in the rest of the batter. Fold over the overhanging filo pastry so that it sits on the surface. Take the remaining filo sheets one at a time, brush with melted butter, crumple them up gently and place them on top of the cake but leaving the center exposed.

Place the springform pan on a cookie sheet and place in the preheated oven. Bake for 20 minutes. Lower the oven temperature to 325°F. Bake for an additional 1 hour and 15 minutes until it's set and not wet and shiny in the center. If the filo is browning too much, tent it lightly with a sheet of foil. Turn off the oven and leave the cheesecake for 30 minutes to cool slowly. Remove and allow to cool at room temperature for several hours before serving. Loosen from the sides of the pan and place on a serving platter. Garnish with a drizzle of rose syrup and chopped pistachios.

Baraziq are a cross between a pastry and a cookie. They are delicate and melt in your mouth.
Clarifying the butter gives them a unique taste and texture. Place two of these cookies alongside my
"Thousand and One Nights" ice cream (recipe on page 145) for added crunch.

Sesame and Pistachio Nut Cookies (Baraziq)

Makes 5 dozen cookies

1 cup sesame seeds (lightly toasted)
½ cup clarified butter, chilled • ½ cup icing sugar
1 egg • 1 tsp vanilla • 1 tsp vinegar
1½ cups flour • 1 tsp baking powder
pinch of salt • 1 cup pistachios, sliced thinly
½ cup milk

Toast the sesame seeds by placing the seeds in a large dry frying pan on medium heat. Stir continuously until the sesame seeds become toasted and lightly golden. Place on a shallow pan to cool completely.

In a bowl beat the butter and icing sugar using an electric mixer until pale and creamy. Add the egg, vanilla and vinegar and beat for 2 more minutes. Sift the flour, baking powder and salt together and add to the creamed mixture to form a dough that is pliable but not sticky. Cover and place in the fridge for half an hour to rest before shaping the cookies.

Preheat the oven to 350°F.

Prepare your workstation by placing the toasted sesame seeds in a shallow bowl and the pistachio nuts in another. Pour the milk into a third bowl. Pinch a piece of dough the size of a large marble and flatten in your hand. Dip your fingers of the other hand in the milk and dab one side of the cookie and press into the pistachios first. Do the same on the other side and press into the sesame seeds. Be firm yet gentle as they are delicate. Place on a parchment-lined pan and bake for approximately 12 minutes until lightly golden and crisp. Remove and cool before storing in an airtight container.

These cookies have no eggs or baking powder in them. It is essential that you beat the clarified butter and sugar well. This is the secret to their unique texture. They are meltingly smooth on the outside with a delicate crunch on the inside. They are very easy to make, but it is important to work with a gentle hand to ensure the dough remains light and fluffy.

Arabic Shortbread

Makes 6 dozen cookies

**1 cup clarified butter, chilled • ¾ cup icing sugar
1 tsp vanilla • 1½ cups flour
pinch of salt • pine nuts, to garnish**

In a medium bowl beat together the clarified butter and sugar using an electric mixer for about 10 minutes, until pale and creamy. Add the vanilla. Mix well. Sift the flour and salt and add gradually to the beaten mixture. Test the dough by seeing if you can roll a ball in your hand without sticking. Beat on low speed until it comes together. Cover and refrigerate for 30 minutes before shaping the shortbread.

Preheat the oven to 325°F.

Take small-sized pieces of the dough and roll gently in the palms of your hand to make a ball the size of a large marble. Place on a parchment-lined baking sheet. Gently flatten into a disk and press a pine nut into the center. Bake for 10–12 minutes until it just sets. Don't let the cookies brown; they should remain an ivory color. Remove and leave to cool completely on the tray before serving.

Knafe Nabulsieh is the ultimate special-occasion dessert of the Arab world and is the undisputed specialty of Nablus, where the famous white sheep's milk cheese is made. It is served at the happiest of times: weddings, engagements, the birth of a baby, graduation, and the welcoming home of loved ones. I once made it to celebrate my daughter's first birthday instead of the usual birthday cake. The orange color is a traditional touch and looks beautiful with the green pistachios on top. One bite of the crisp, buttery pastry and oozing cheese sweetened with the fragrant syrup is absolutely heavenly.

Knafe Pastry with Cheese

8-10 servings

1 pkg (1 lb) knafe (or "kataife") pastry, thawed • 1 cup clarified butter, melted and still hot
2 lb Nabulsieh or akkawi cheese, desalted • ½ lb fresh mozzarella cheese
6 Tbsp sugar • 2 Tbsp orange blossom water • 2 Tbsp rosewater
¼ cup clarified butter • 4 drops of orange food coloring paste

3 cups rose syrup (see recipe on page 181)
1 cup ground pistachios, to garnish

In a food processor begin to grind the pastry, keeping it coarse. Do this in four batches. Place in a large bowl and pour the hot clarified butter on top. Using your hands, rub the butter to coat every strand of pastry. Set aside.

In a colander, drain the desalted cheese and pat dry with a tea towel. Add the mozzarella cheese. Sprinkle the sugar on top followed by the orange blossom water and rosewater. Mix together well.

Preheat the oven to 375°F.

Coat a 10- to 12-inch-round baking pan or pie plate with the butter. Add the orange food coloring in the bottom of the pan and use a piece of wax paper to spread the color and butter all over and up the sides of the pan. Take handfuls of the buttered pastry and press into the prepared pan, going slightly up the sides. Use approximately two-thirds of the pastry mixture. Place the prepared cheese on top, pressing to cover completely. Place a couple of paper towels on the cheese to absorb any excess water. Cover with the remaining pastry and press gently. Bake in the preheated oven for approximately 40 minutes until the cheese melts and the pastry becomes crisp. Give it a shake – the knafe will come away from the sides in one piece. Remove and invert the hot knafe onto a serving platter with the orange side on top. Douse with the cooled syrup. Garnish with the ground pistachio nuts. Indulge while it's hot.

The holidays just wouldn't be the same without these delicate filled pastries on the table. They are made on special occasions like Eid Al-Fitr and Easter. It is one dough filled with three different fillings. It takes a little time to prepare these pastries but is well worth it. I usually bake a big batch, and freeze some in an airtight container. They keep well in the freezer. I have given instructions to decorate the pastries using decorative pinchers. After a couple of attempts you'll get the hang of it. Alternatively, you can use special molds.

Pistachio, Walnut and Date Pastries (Maamoul)

Makes approx. 100 pastries

Pistachio Filling
1 cup pistachios, chopped
5 Tbsp sugar
1 Tbsp rosewater
1 Tbsp orange blossom water

Walnut Filling
1 cup walnuts, chopped medium fine
5 Tbsp sugar
2 Tbsp orange blossom water
zest of ½ orange
1 tsp cinnamon

Date Filling
2 cups chopped pitted dates
1 Tbsp ground nutmeg
1 Tbsp melted butter

2 lb (6 cups) fine semolina
2 Tbsp ground mahlab
3 cups clarified butter, melted
1 tsp instant dry yeast
1 Tbsp sugar
2 cups full-fat milk, lukewarm
icing sugar for dusting

Prepare each filling by mixing the ingredients in a bowl. For the date filling, knead the dates with the nutmeg and butter until soft. (You can warm the dates in the oven to make them easier to knead.) Break off a piece and roll into a log about 4 inches long. Bring the ends together to form a 1½-inch-diameter ring. Proceed until all are done and set aside.

In a large bowl put the semolina, mahlab and sugar and mix well. Pour in the melted butter and mix in with your fingertips, coating completely. Sprinkle on the yeast and sugar to incorporate. Gradually pour in the slightly warmed milk and mix until the mixture forms a dough. It should be soft and pliable, and not sticky. You may not end up using all of the milk.

For the nut-filled maamoul, take a piece of dough of about the size of a walnut and cup it in one hand. With your thumb poke the center of the dough to make a well. Using your thumb on the inside and your index finger on the outside, work the dough upwards to thin it out gradually into a shell. Place a teaspoonful of the nut filling in the well. Bring the edges together to cover the filling completely. Smooth out and turn over the filled pastry. With a pincher proceed to decorate the shell. Make your pistachio-filled ones oval and your walnut-filled ones round. Place on a baking sheet.

For the date-filled maamoul, take a walnut-sized piece of dough and flatten in the palm of your hand. Place a prepared date ring in the center and fold the edges over to enclose completely toward the center. Follow the shape of the date ring and pinch the center to make a hole in the middle. It will look like a filled donut. Turn the seam side down. Grab hold of the pastry in one hand and proceed to use the pincher to decorate (see inset). Place on a baking sheet.

Preheat oven to 375°F. Bake for about 15–20 minutes. The maamoul should only be slightly colored. Remove and cool completely before dusting with icing sugar. Store cooled pastries in an airtight container without the icing sugar.

Batheeth is a specialty of the United Arab Emirates and many of the countries of the Gulf. It is a clever way of making a pastry without the use of an oven (something that was lacking in the deserts long ago). I roll out the dough and cut it into shapes. And then the best is yet to come, a squiggly drizzle of melted chocolate to bring it to another level. Pour a demitasse of fragrant Arabic coffee and enjoy.

Date Pastries (Batheeth)

Makes 5 dozen pastries

½ cup clarified butter • ½ tsp nutmeg
½ tsp ground cardamom • 1½ cups flour
3 cups chopped pitted dates (soft like medjool)
10 oz dark chocolate (70% cocoa), in pieces

In a small saucepan melt the butter, add the nutmeg and cardamom and set aside.

Place the flour in a heavy saucepan on medium heat and begin to toast the flour until it browns lightly, stirring continuously.

When the flour is ready add the dates and continue to mix until the dates soften. Pour the warm melted butter on top of the flour/date mixture and mix well. When cool enough to handle but still quite warm, turn out and knead slightly to make a dough. Roll out on a working surface, and use a cookie cutter to cut into desired shapes. I used a 2-inch heart shape for the photo. Place on a parchment-lined baking sheet.

For the chocolate, simmer water in a saucepan. Put a heat-resistant bowl on top but not touching the water. Pour in the chocolate pieces and leave to melt slowly. Stir well, remove from the heat and drizzle a squiggle on each cookie. Set aside to set.

Rice pudding is one of those desserts that cuts across all cultures. Cooking milk, sugar and rice together is very simple yet very tasty. I've flavored it with fresh vanilla beans and given it a twist by adding a date compote. The sweet dates complement the creaminess of the pudding. This is another one of those comfort foods my mother made often when I was young. I always burned my tongue eating it because I couldn't wait for it to cool!

Rice Pudding with Date Compote

6–8 servings

3 Tbsp cornstarch • ½ cup cold milk • 5 cups full-fat milk
1 cup heavy cream • 1 vanilla pod, split and scraped
1 cup short-grain white rice, presoaked and drained • 1 cup sugar
1 Tbsp rosewater • 1 Tbsp orange blossom water

½ cup water • ¼ cup sugar • 1 cup dates, pitted and chopped
½ cup orange juice • zest of ½ orange • juice of ½ lemon
½ cup pistachios, chopped

Make a paste by combining the cornstarch and cold milk and set aside. In a large heavy-bottomed saucepan heat the 5 cups milk and the cream. Slice the vanilla pod lengthwise; with the back of a knife scrape the seeds and add to the hot milk and cream along with the pod. Allow to come to a boil. Add the drained rice and stir with a wooden spoon continuously until the rice cooks and the mixture thickens slightly, about 20–25 minutes. Add the sugar and continue stirring. Pour in the cornstarch/milk paste and stir in one direction as it thickens for about 2 minutes. Remove from the heat and take out the vanilla pod. Stir in the rosewater and orange blossom water. Set aside.

To make the compote, heat the water and sugar in a small saucepan until the sugar dissolves. Add the dates, orange juice, orange zest and lemon juice and allow to come to a boil. Lower the heat to a simmer and leave until the dates soften. Remove from the heat and allow to cool. Half-fill individual clear glass cups with rice pudding, cover and cool in the fridge. When ready to serve, put a dollop of the date compote on top and garnish with chopped pistachio nuts.

I don't remember my mother making us a dessert on a daily basis. Desserts were for holidays and special occasions. Instead we would sit around every evening while my mother peeled and cut what seemed an endless amount of fruit while she shared with us stories like how much better fruit tasted "back home," freshly picked and in season. She was on a never-ending quest to find a pear that wasn't, in her words, "tasteless." As she talked we listened and watched in amazement how she peeled an orange in one long continuous strip. This fruit salad is a combination of all the fruit she loves. They are all similar in texture and easy to scoop into balls. Of course you can use your favorite fruit and cut it the way you like. I've included cactus fruit if you can find it. I did manage to find a sweet, ripe pear as well. My mother would be delighted!

Fruit Salad

6-8 servings

Yogurt Honey Sauce
1 cup full-fat yogurt • ½ cup heavy cream, whipped slightly to thicken
¼ cup honey • 1 vanilla bean, scraped

½ cup cantaloupe • ½ cup honeydew melon
½ cup watermelon • 2 mangoes • 3 kiwis
4 cactus fruit • 2 ripe pears
½ cup rose syrup (see recipe on page 181)
1 cup fresh pomegranate seeds, to garnish
½ cup chopped pistachios, presoaked in 3 Tbsp rosewater, to garnish

In a bowl place the yogurt, the slightly thickened cream and honey. Slice the vanilla bean in half, scrape the seeds and place in the bowl. Whisk together to combine and set aside. Using a melon baller, scoop out balls of each fruit.

Put in a large bowl and mix gently to combine. Place in individual serving dishes and drizzle on some rose syrup. Garnish with the fresh pomegranate seeds and pistachio nuts. Serve alongside the yogurt honey sauce.

This is an exotic flavored milk pudding called m'hallabiya, one of our classic desserts.
I paired it with apricot but it is equally as delicious with a date or fig compote.

Milk Pudding with Apricot Compote

6–8 servings

Apricot Compote
½ cup apricot jam • 8 dried apricots, finely sliced
zest of ½ orange • juice of ½ orange • juice of ½ lemon

4 cups full-fat milk • 1 cup sugar
¼ cup cornstarch mixed with ¼ cup milk to make a paste
½ tsp mastic ground with 1 Tbsp sugar
1 tsp rosewater • 1 Tbsp orange blossom water
toasted slivered almonds, to garnish
fresh pomegranate seeds, to garnish

In a small saucepan, combine all the ingredients to make the compote and heat gently on low heat while stirring for about 5 minutes. Taste. Set aside to cool.

Over medium heat, pour the milk and sugar in a large saucepan and stir until the sugar has dissolved. Add the cornstarch paste to the hot milk and whisk to combine. Bring to a boil and stir until thickened (it should coat the back of a spoon). Remove from the heat, add the mastic/sugar mixture, rosewater and orange blossom water and mix well. Allow to cool slightly before serving.

To assemble, place a heaped spoonful of the apricot compote in individual clear glasses. Carefully ladle the m'hallabiya on top, taking care not to mix it with the compote. Garnish with toasted almonds and fresh pomegranate seeds. Cover with plastic wrap and cool in the fridge until ready to serve.

I started making these cookies for Eman, my oldest daughter, when she was two years old. On our excursions to the park, we would meet many mothers and babies. Eman would be munching on these cookies and catch the attention of other children asking for a bite. I've passed out this recipe to many loving mothers who wanted to make something more wholesome for their families. Baking with my children is one of my favorite things to do. After many messy baking sessions and experimenting with various shapes and letters, they decided that the "S" was the winner, and the cookies were officially named "S" cookies.

Date-Filled "S" Cookies

Makes about 50 cookies

4 cups flour • 1 Tbsp mahlab • pinch of salt
2 Tbsp sugar • 1 cup clarified butter
1 Tbsp instant dry yeast • 1½ cups warm full-fat milk
3 cups chopped pitted dates kneaded with 2 Tbsp melted butter
2 egg whites • ¼ cup milk • 1 cup raw sesame seeds

In a large bowl, mix the flour, mahlab, salt and sugar together. Add the butter and mix by hand until fully coated. Sprinkle in the yeast and start to pour in the warm milk gradually until absorbed and the dough comes together and pulls away from the sides of the bowl (you may not need all the milk). Knead the dough gently in the bowl, cover and set aside for 30 minutes to allow the dough to rise.

Preheat the oven to 375°F.

Roll the kneaded dates into long logs about the width of your index finger. Take a small piece of dough (roughly the size of a walnut) and flatten into a rectangle with your fingertips on your working surface. Break off a piece of the date filling (about 3 inches), and place on the flattened dough. Fold the dough around the date filling and seal. Ensure it is fully enclosed and shape the cookie into an "S."

Beat the egg whites with the milk in a shallow bowl. Put the sesame seeds in another bowl. Dip one side of the filled cookie in the egg wash and then in the sesame seeds and place on a baking sheet. Bake in the preheated oven until lightly golden, about 15 minutes. Perfect with a cup of tea anytime.

Dates (tamr in Arabic) are enjoyed and cherished like no other fruit in the Arab world. They were once sustenance for the people living in the harsh desert lands. Dates are used to add sweetness to savory rice dishes, and in the UAE, partnered with grilled and fried fish. Dates are made into jam, and used as a stuffing in pastries. Welcome your friends the traditional way with a platter of these decadent dates, and of course a tiny cup of fragrant Arabic coffee anytime of the day.

Spiced Ricotta-Stuffed Dates

Makes 22 dates

22 top-quality dates (such as medjools)
22 blanched almonds
1 cup ricotta cheese • ½ cup mascarpone cheese
¼ cup half-and-half or heavy cream • 1½ tsp freshly grated nutmeg
½ tsp ground cardamom
¼ cup ground pistachios, to garnish

Slice each date lengthwise to remove the pit and open them for the stuffing. Set aside.

Preheat the oven to 375°F.

Place the blanched almonds on a baking sheet and roast in the hot oven just until lightly golden. Remove and cool. Place an almond inside each one of the dates.

In a bowl place the ricotta cheese, mascarpone, cream, nutmeg and cardamom and whisk to combine well. Place in a pastry bag with a thin star-shaped nozzle and fill each date, exposing the filling. Arrange on a nice platter. Garnish with a pinch of chopped pistachios. A perfect sweet finish to any meal.

conversion charts

Weight

1 oz	25 g
2 oz	50 g
3 oz	75 g
4 oz	125 g
5 oz	150 g
6 oz	175 g
7 oz	200 g
8 oz (½ lb)	250 g
9 oz	275 g
10 oz	300 g
11 oz	325 g
12 oz	375 g
13 oz	400 g
14 oz	425 g
15 oz	475 g
16 oz (1 lb)	500 g
2 lb	1 kg

Length

¼ inch	5 mm
½ inch	1 cm
¾ inch	1.5 cm
1 inch	2.5 cm
2 inches	5 cm
3 inches	7 cm
4 inches	10 cm
5 inches	12 cm
6 inches	15 cm
7 inches	18 cm
8 inches	20 cm
9 inches	23 cm
10 inches	25 cm
11 inches	28 cm
12 inches	30 cm

Volume

1 tsp	5 mL	
1 Tbsp	15 mL	
¼ cup	60 mL	2 fl oz
⅓ cup	80 mL	2½ fl oz
½ cup	125 mL	4 fl oz
⅔ cup	160 mL	5 fl oz (¼ pint)
¾ cup	180 mL	6 fl oz
1 cup	250 mL	8 fl oz
1 quart	1 L	

Deep-Frying Temperatures

350°F	177°C
375°F	190°C

Oven Temperatures

Fahrenheit	Celsius	Gas	Description
225°F	110°C	¼	Cool
250°F	130°C	½	Cool
275°F	140°C	1	Very low
300°F	150°C	2	Very low
325°F	170°C	3	Low
350°F	180°C	4	Moderate
375°F	190°C	5	Moderate/hot
400°F	200°C	6	Hot
425°F	220°C	7	Hot
450°F	230°C	8	Very hot
475°F	240°C	9	Very hot

• For fan assisted ovens: reduce the temperature by 20°F/10°C

basic recipes

■■

Clarified Butter

Cookies and pastries made with clarified butter will keep longer because the milk solids have separated from the butter. It also gives food a unique texture and flavor.

Place 2 lb (4 cups) of unsalted butter in a large enough saucepan and place on medium heat. Let it come to a rolling boil and let it continue boiling on a gentle heat. Remove the foam that comes to the surface and discard. When the butter becomes clear and no longer foggy and the milk solids have settled to the bottom, turn the heat off. Allow the clarified butter to cool completely. Pour through a sieve to strain any particles before storing in a clean glass jar for later use. It will keep for a month at room temperature and longer in the fridge.

Rose (or Simple) Syrup
2 cups sugar • 1 cup water
1 Tbsp lemon juice • 1 tsp rosewater
1 tsp orange blossom water

Make the simple syrup by combing the sugar and water in a medium-sized saucepan over medium-high heat. Add the lemon juice and allow to boil for 5 minutes. Lower the heat and simmer for an additional 5 minutes. Remove from the heat to cool and stir in the rosewater and orange blossom water. Store in a clean sealable glass jar.

Labneh
Makes about 3 cups

5 quarts whole milk (20 cups)
2 cups plain full-fat milk yogurt (starter)
salt • large piece of cheesecloth, a double layer

Start this process 2 nights before you plan to use the labneh. Pour all of the milk in a large deep pot and place on a medium heat. Allow the milk to almost come up to boil. Remove from the heat and leave to cool to lukewarm temperature. You should be able to immerse your hand in the milk with no discomfort.

When the milk is ready, stir in the 2 cups of yogurt. Make sure that it has melted throughout. Cover the pot. Place in a dark, draft-free area. Wrap with a blanket and leave undisturbed overnight. In the morning you will wake up to a pot of fresh yogurt. Refrigerate the yogurt for at least 6 hours to set properly. Now it is ready to eat or turn into labneh. At this point I like to add the salt to the yogurt. Mix well. Place the doubled cheesecloth on a large enough colander and begin to ladle the yogurt. It looks like a lot at this point but when all the water is drained you will be left with about 3 cups of labneh. Twist and tie the cloth well. I tie it to my kitchen tap and allow the excess water to drip all night. Or you could leave it in the colander and place it in a bigger bowl to drain. Place a weight on top to hurry the process, and keep throwing out the water that collects in the bowl. At this point you can decide how thick you want your labneh to be. It should at least be a dipping consistency. If you want to make the labneh balls on page 53 (in the mezze chapter), dry out the labneh further to the consistency of goat cheese.

arabic ingredients and tools

Akkawi Cheese – A white salty cheese, similar to halloumi, used in many Arabic sweets. It needs to be desalted before using. It can be found in all Middle Eastern grocery stores. Mozzarella is a good substitute.

Bulgur – Wheat that has been boiled, dried and cracked. It can be ground either fine or coarse, the former being the best for making *kibbeh nayye* and tabbouleh and the latter best used in pilafs or as a stuffing. Bulgur is very nutritious and used to be the main grain eaten all over the Middle East before rice was introduced to the region.

Cardamom – A pungent spice used commonly all around the Middle East. The pods are usually green on the outside with small black seeds on the inside that are ground finely and can be used in many sweet and savory dishes. Cardamom gives the classic Arabic coffee its unique taste.

Cilantro (or coriander) – A herb that resembles parsley but has a citrusy and pungent taste. Very commonly used to enhance stews, in salads and sauces.

Dried Fava Beans – They come in two forms: *ful makshoor* has been split with the peel removed and dried. This is the bean used to make falafel. The other is *ful*, which is whole and has a brown outer skin. *Ful* is soaked overnight and cooked slowly until it is meltingly soft for use in the dish *ful m'dammas*. Canned, precooked fava beans are also readily available in all Middle Eastern grocery stores.

Extra Virgin Olive Oil – People of the Mediterranean have a lot in common and olive oil is the liquid gold that is virtually indispensable to all. The tastiest is the first-pressed extra virgin olive oil; it tastes fruity and is best for drizzling over any food to bring out the flavors. A lighter oil can be used for light cooking and sautéing.

Falafel Utensil – Found in most Middle Eastern stores to form a uniform falafel patty. It has a lever that you press down to form the falafel and release to drop in the hot oil. Two spoons dipped in oil can be a good substitute if you cannot find this tool.

Filo – A pastry that is thin as paper and sold frozen. It needs to be thawed in the fridge overnight before using. Layers of filo contribute to baklawa's distinct crispiness.

Freekeh –Wheat that goes through a different process than bulgur. The green wheat stalks are harvested and roasted on an open fire to create a distinct smoky flavor. Pick over and rinse well before using since there may be stones and other debris hidden within. Keep stored in a dry sealed container in the fridge to prevent it from going rancid.

Grapevine Leaves – Mostly sold packed in brine in jars and available in all Middle Eastern stores. After removing, rinse well with cold water and trim the stalks before using. Grapevine leaves can be used in both meat and vegetarian dishes.

Jute Mallow (Mloukhiya) – A leafy vegetable resembling mint in appearance. It is part of the jute family. It has an earthy green taste and is cooked as part of a chicken or lamb stew.

Kibbeh Spice Mix – A combination of spices commonly used in making *kibbeh* whether it's served in tartare form (*kibbeh nayye*) or fried or baked. It usually includes cumin, allspice, cinnamon, marjoram, baby rose petals, black pepper and cloves.

Labneh – The result of straining plain yogurt in a cheesecloth for a long period of time. When all of the water is extracted the labneh will be as thick as cream cheese but lower in fat.

Maamoul Molds – Decorative molds made of wood or sometimes plastic. They are used to press the *maamoul* pastry so it takes on a pattern before baking. A light tap on the working surface will drop the decorated pastry right side up.

Mahlab – A unique spice added to pastries and other sweet baked goods. It is the ground kernel found inside the pits of black cherries. Always buy it whole and grind in small quantities and store in the freezer.

Mastic – It is an aromatic resin from a tree. It can be used as a flavoring in sweet or savory dishes. It is the secret flavor in traditional Arabic ice cream.

Nabulsieh Cheese – A sheep's milk cheese that is the specialty of Nablus, Palestine. Mahlab and/or mastic is added to the milk during the cooking process and gives it its characteristic taste. The cheese is boiled and preserved in very salty water. To use in recipes, it needs to be soaked in a few changes of water.

Okra – Baby okra is most often used in Arabic dishes. It is tender and doesn't have the seeds found in the larger okra. While finding fresh okra is sometimes challenging, the frozen variety is just as good. All Middle Eastern grocery stores carry frozen baby okra and you should find regular frozen okra at your local supermarket.

Orange Blossom Water – This fragrant water is distilled from the blossoms of Seville oranges. Use sparingly to add an unforgettable smell and taste to so many dishes. It can be combined with rosewater for a unique flavor.

Pastry Pinchers – A small pincer with two serrated edges used to decorate *maamoul* pastries by making indentations in a decorative pattern.

Pomegranate Molasses – Sour pomegranate juice is boiled and reduced to a thick and dark syrup (like a balsamic vinegar reduction). It's used to flavor meats, salads and stews, adding a nice lift to any dish. It should be used sparingly as its tartness is very strong.

Purslane – The purslane leaves are small, delicate and round in shape. They can be cooked and used as a succulent filling or eaten raw as part of a salad. If you can't find it at a Middle Eastern grocery store, try a Mexican grocery store where purslane is sold as *verdolaga*. Watercress and arugula can work as substitutes.

Rosewater – A fragrant water distilled from pink rose petals known as *ward el jouri* in Arabic. It is mostly used as a flavoring in puddings, drinks and sweet pastries. Even savory rice dishes are sometimes infused with rosewater.

Saffron – The deep orange stigmas from a special purple crocus. It is labor-intensive to collect therefore it is very expensive. It adds a beautiful yellow color and a floral flavor to dishes and is often added to rice near the end of cooking.

Sahleb – Authentic sahleb is a powder extracted from the tubers of wild orchids. Sahleb and sahleb substitutes are used as a thickening agent to make the classic Arabic ice cream and are also the secret behind its elasticity. Boiled with milk and sugar, sahleb thickens to make a popular hot drink enjoyed all over the Middle East.

Semolina – Made from hard durum wheat, it is ground either coarse or fine, the latter being the best for delicate pastries like *maamoul*. The coarse semolina is best for *nammoura* cake.

Simple Syrup – A syrup used to sweeten so many Arabic pastries. Known by the name *ater* or *sheera*, the syrup is usually made fragrant with the addition of rosewater and orange blossom water or a combination of the two.

Sumac – A crimson-red spice used often in Middle Eastern cuisine. It comes from the sumac berriy. It has a distinct sour taste and adds some color as well. It is also one of the main ingredients in the *za'atar* spice mixture.

Tahini – 100% ground raw sesame seeds are the only ingredients in a jar of tahini. Beware of imposters that mix in peanuts. Tahini is one of the most important ingredients in an Arabic kitchen. There would be no hummus without it. It adds a rich, nutty taste to many savory dishes and desserts as well. Keep stored in the fridge. The oil will separate if not used often. Should this happen, just stir it vigorously.

Taklia – Garlic and fresh cilantro sautéed in a little butter or oil and added to a dish near the end of cooking to add flavor.

Wild Thyme – A popular herb and the main ingredient of the dry spice mixture *za'atar*. The thyme that is widely available in the Middle East – *Thymbra spicata* or *Thymus capitatus* – is slightly different from the common varieties of thyme in North America. It is used fresh to enhance yogurt, labneh, soups and roasted meats; on its own it makes a delicious salad. The best substitute in terms of flavor and texture is fresh oregano.

Za'atar – The mixture of dried thyme, ground sumac, salt and toasted sesame seeds. Served as a dry condiment alongside some fruity extra virgin olive oil. Mixed together it makes a nice filling for croissants and of course, *manaqeesh za'atar* (za'atar flatbread).

index

acknowledgments

Where does one begin to thank the many people who had a hand in making this dream of mine a reality? I like to call them my dream team.

Thank you, Jonathan Griffiths, for setting this dream in motion. For my dear friend Perla Lichi for your continued love and support and for showing me there is more to a number than you think. Many thanks to Wakami Saab for your never-ending generosity. For Najat Al Sayyed, you are truly a special friend. Thank you, Maria Norman, for never giving up and for being so supportive. For Stephanie Mahmoud, whose joy and enthusiasm make it an absolute pleasure to work with her. For Isobel Abulhoul for believing in me and inspiring me to soar a little higher, thank you for being a special part of my journey.

The saying goes that a picture is worth a thousand words. Truly the stunning photography speaks volumes. Petrina, thank you for capturing my food in the most beautiful way. And to my food stylist extraordinaire, Alison Attenborough. Thank you, Leanna Maione, for your hard work and also for keeping teatime alive.

I am grateful for the generosity of so many people from various stores who offered us gorgeous props for the photo shoot. Thank you, Bloomingdale's, Tavola, O'de Rose, Harvest Home, Zara, Asala, Geneviève Lethu and Perla Lichi Design.

Thank you, Jane Hodges, Maram Borno, Sundos Shaikhly, Victoria Crick, Tarek Tawil, Erika Oliveira, Kathy Santiago, Lucy Taylor, Caroline, Denise Roig and Josephine.

Robert, fate brought us together and I am so grateful that you loved my food so much. Looking forward to our cooking sessions. Grace, thank you for all the care and attention you put in your work and gracing every page with your perfect points. Thank you, Lindsay, for being a valuable part of this book. My sincere thanks to Anna Olson, Lynn Crawford and Bal Arneson for pointing me in the right direction.

Then there are my "Girls," Tala Duwaji, Gaby Tulipano and Lana Makhzoumi, who were always ready to taste and critique my food. Thank you, my dear friend Jehanne Aswad, for always being there. Thank you, Nadine Qonso, for the privilege of letting me wear your beautiful one-of-a-kind jewelry at my photo shoot. Thanks, Anne, Jenny, Stephanie and Melanie, for your encouragement.

I have been so fortunate to have met so many wonderful people in my life. Thank you to all of my friends I've made along the way who have graced my table. Cooking for you has been a true joy. My heartfelt thanks to all of the fans of my show *Sohbe Taibe*. Your kind words and continued support have meant so much to me.

A big hug for my dear son, Mahmoud, who tirelessly worked with me and put up with my endless tweaking. Thank you to all of my family for your love and encouragement. My never-ending love and admiration to you, Ahmed, for managing to keep up with all of my dreams. And to my children, Eman, Mahmoud and Mimi, who are the reason why I cook with love.

Finally, to Scott Messina: Our paths crossed for a reason. I will always be grateful to you for your encouragement and generosity.